52 THINGS KIDS NEED FROM A MOM

ANGELA THOMAS

HARVEST HOUSE PUBLISHERS

EUGENE, OREGON

Cover photo © iStockphoto / Thinkstock

Cover design by Koechel Peterson & Associates, Inc., Minneapolis, Minnesota

Published in association with BrandWaves LLC, Brentwood, TN 37027. www.brandwavesllc.com

52 THINGS KIDS NEED FROM A MOM
Copyright © 2011 by Angela Thomas
Published by Harvest House Publishers
Eugene, Oregon 97402
www.harvesthousepublishers.com

Library of Congress Cataloging-in-Publication Data
   Thomas, Angela
   52 things kids need from a mom / Angela Thomas.
      p. cm.
   ISBN 978-0-7369-4391-8 (pbk.)
   ISBN 978-0-7369-4392-5 (eBook)
   1. Mother and child—Religious aspects—Christianity. I. Title.
   BV4529.18.T449 2011
   248.8'431—dc22

                                              2011014612

Printed in the United States of America

11 12 13 14 15 16 17 18 / VP-SK / 10 9 8 7 6 5 4 3 2 1

For
Taylor, Grayson, William, and AnnaGrace.

More than all these things, I give you my love.
I will adore you forever and ever.
Mom

Acknowledgments

A very special thanks to my husband, Scott Pharr. Because you are by my side, loving these beautiful children with me, I am learning more about what it means to be their mom. You have given strength and stability to our home. You make every day fun and set the tone of our home with your consistent good attitude and humor. Your selfless spirit and compassionate heart challenge me to become more like you. Because you lead us with godliness, I too want to keep growing, taking every next step toward greater maturity in Christ. The children and I love you deeply. So much of this book, I have learned from you.

Thank you to LaRae Weikert for thinking of me to write this book. What a privilege to partner with Harvest House for this message! Thank you to Bob Hawkins and Terry Glaspey for your encouragement and work alongside me.

And mostly, to my Savior, Jesus. You have carried this broken mom. Healed my broken kids. Restored my broken home. Mended my broken heart. If I could only give one thing to my kids, it would be You. Thank You for everlasting love.

Contents

From Angela

Dear mom like me,

Tonight as I write to you, I am praying for you and for your children. Oh, how you have such a tender place in my heart. Being a mom is the greatest privilege that has come to me, and I know you feel the same way. It is such an honor to meet you here in these pages and share a bit of our journey together.

I want you to know that I have written these 52 things as prompts. Ideas. Creative reminders. Two of my girlfriends read the contents page for this book, and both of them called me to say, "I haven't done even half of them. I hope there's still time left." So I want to tell you what I told them: "There is no guilt in these pages. They have not been written as a checklist for women who want to be impressive moms. Each of these chapters was written out of longing, desire, and love."

Some of you could write 1052 *other* things kids need from a mom. My friend with an autistic son could help us all learn so much more about patience and championing your child. My friend with adopted children would be able to give us lists of things kids need to adapt to a new culture and make the transition from orphanage to family. Another one of my friends spends almost every moment caring for her baby, who has had life-threatening issues and too many stays in the hospital. Oh, the things she could tell us.

The point is that we are each on a different journey, but we all long to love our children well, to be great moms, and to become even better along the way. I am praying that in these pages you find encouragement, renewed inspiration, and hope. I pray that you can laugh at yourself, and your kids, when necessary. I pray for you and for myself that when we know better, we'll do better. I am not done yet. I still want to become the mom God had in mind when He entrusted four beautiful children to me.

Before you jump into the chapters, I just want to give you the pre-thing before the 52 things. This is the biggie that matters more than all the rest: *Love*.

Love those kids with all your heart, soul, and might. Love them through their mistakes. Love them in their changes. Love them when they're dorky. Love them when they are accomplished. Just open your heart and don't hold back...ever. Our children need one person on this earth who will love them fiercely, no matter what this life holds. That task has been assigned to you and me. So let us learn to love with a healthy love. A godly love. A mushy love. A powerful, transforming love.

And so my friend, welcome to *52 Things Kids Need from a Mom*. May God add His grace to these pages and His wisdom to our hearts. I have nothing to offer apart from Him.

Let's love those pumpkins like crazy and enjoy every single day we have been given.

It's a privilege to be a mom alongside you today,

Angela

Kids Need Their Mom...

To Pray in Secret
with the Door Open

In my first years as a mom, I desperately wanted to keep a passionate spiritual life with God. I wanted to read the Bible. Sit quietly and pray. Maybe even write a few things in my journal. It's just that my little people would not cooperate. I had four babies in seven years, and not one of them was willing to go along with my plan. My heart kept longing to go back and have a spiritual life the way I'd always had. Alone. It took me a while to realize that being a mom means you might never be alone again.

Frustrated. Probably even mad sometimes. I remember shaking my head and just fussing on the inside about my crazy, chaotic predicament. *I am trying to be with God so that I can be a better mom. Anybody with me here?* As you can imagine, being alone rarely happened. And I'd feel guilty about my crumbling spiritual life. And the only ones I knew to blame were *them*, the ones I loved so dearly, who needed me every minute.

I'd love to tell you that the answer for my struggle came to me in a moment of brilliance. But I was too tired to be brilliant. There was just an afternoon. I think I put on a video for the kids to watch and went upstairs to my bedroom. For some reason I kept the door open and sat down on the floor to read my Bible for a minute, and then I stretched out, facedown, on my carpet to pray. I guess I had been praying for one whole minute, and then they came.

I could hear them coming down the hall, but that day, instead of stopping what I was doing, I just kept lying there, praying. Of course, they walked right in, and I'm sure you can guess what they did. They crawled on top of me. And they played with my hair. And they wiggled their little faces up to mine.

"Hey, mama," one whispered.

"Hey, honey," a gentle, not frustrated, voice spoke from inside of me.

"Watcha doin'?" they said in unison.

"Praying."

"Oh…it looked like you were sleeping," an honest observer said.

It's been known to happen, I admitted to myself.

Do you know what they did next? Those little toddling children lay down beside me and mostly of on top of me and prayed too. Oh, they prayed squirrelly prayers that lasted for only a couple of minutes, but they prayed. My babies were praying because they had seen their mama praying.

> I heard God speaking to me, "I want your kids to see you being with Me."

After a few minutes they were done, but I just kept lying there while they ran in and out. Back to the video. Then back to check on praying mom. And God settled something inside of me that afternoon. The days of being a college coed with lots of time to be alone to pray were over. That chapter was closed. And honestly, I didn't want to go back. I just longed for the sweetness of how I used to spend time with God.

But lying on my bedroom floor that day, I knew I heard Him speaking to me:

> This is how I want you to pray now. Pray in secret—with the door open. I want them to see you being with Me. I want them to catch you turning to your heavenly Father for guidance. I want them to learn from you how to walk with Me. No dramatic presentation needed. No fanfare required. Angela, this is a new season with a new way. And this new way for your heart pleases Me.

I remember being so very humbled. And grateful. My uptight, "everything must be right" personality could have kept me away from God for years. Trying to get it all together. Trying to be just right before I could spend time with Him. But that day God so tenderly walked me step-by-step through one of the most powerful lessons about grace I have ever known.

Come to Me messy.
Come when you're tired.
Let the children lie on top of you.
Let them interrupt you.
You do not have to be perfect...just come to Me and let them see.

A woman stopped me last night. She said she'd heard me tell this story a few years ago and it completely changed her as a mom. She too had been trying to keep the rules and do things neatly, in order, the way she always had. She told me, "I do my Bible study sitting on the bathroom floor while my kids are in the tub. Most of the pages are warped by splashes of water, and some of my notes written in ink run, but those messy, imperfect books are treasures to me now."

My kids are older now, but the lesson remains. They still need to catch me praying. They should walk past my room and know I'm reading my Bible. They need to find the notes I've taken lying on the counter in the kitchen. They need to overhear me praying with a friend on the phone.

I bet your kids do too.

It seems that the lessons we so want to teach our kids are transferred—and not because we sit them down in the living room, pass out ten pages about being spiritual, and then give them a long-winded lecture about how our family is going to follow God. The thing that shapes them more deeply is that you and I pursue God in the everyday of living—that our spiritual lives become the backdrop for their childhood. Bibles left open are normal. A kneeling, praying mom is an ordinary sight. Bibles studies done at bath time, routine.

Reaching Their Hearts

One afternoon I had gone to pray in secret, but God so beautifully taught me that my "secret" needed to be seen. Jesus said in Matthew 6 that we are supposed to keep a secret life. To give in secret, pray in secret, and fast in secret. But I think that when we become moms, for a season those sets of eyes sent from heaven to watch you need to see what you do with God in your "unseen" moments.

May it be so for you and me. And may the children who witness our prayers learn to pray more powerfully because they catch us being with God.

Kids Need Their Mom...

To Never Stop Touching Them

M om, will you tuck me in tonight?" my 17-year-old son accidentally asked me in front of his best friend.

"Dude, what did you just say?" his cool friend asked as he reacted with mock horror and yet with just a little envy.

"Uh…" With a deep voice, the embarrassed one tried to recover a tiny drop of dignity. "I just like my mom to scratch my back before I fall asleep."

The truth is, all of my now-teenage kids like me to scratch their backs, and play with their hair, and just sit on the side of their beds until they can't think of one more thing to tell me.

I love that we have a loving home, but honestly, this kind of affection has been an *intentional* pursuit ever since my first baby was born. I'm afraid that without an everyday choosing, we may have drifted apart—especially as we all learned to navigate their journeys toward separation and independence.

When my children were younger, a man whose name I can't even remember told me, "Never stop touching them. When you walk past your children in the kitchen, reach out and brush their shoulder. When you see them in the morning, hug them and tousle their hair. Touch them every day, many times a day, and never stop."

I am so grateful for that man. He was right. His instructions are, to this day, the foundation for the tender, positive relationships I have with my children. There is affection in our home. These days, I am mostly the initiator, but even in these distance-testing teen years, all of my kids receive my touch, and I can feel the unspoken safety and love it transfers to them.

For the past 20 years, I have tried to do exactly what that man said.

Touch them. I've never talked to them about it, but I imagine that somewhere in their subconscious, when they sense me walk past, something inside of them expects a little pat or a tender rub. I've tried to do that. And if I've been momentarily distracted, I try to go back and make sure they got a touch.

> I have always wanted my touch to say to them, *I am madly in love with you. My love is unconditional. You will never outgrow your mama's love.*

On the days my kids feel quiet or grumpy and obviously need a little space, I try to use fewer words and just put a gentle hand to their shoulder. A little squeeze. A tiny kiss to the forehead. A little reminder that my love is the same. They can talk when they're ready. On their silly days I can hug them like a crazy mama. Crazy-mama hugs, for me, include two arms and one leg wrapped around their gangly legs. I kiss their cheeks and face and hair as though I haven't seen them for years, even if it's only been overnight. Today my 15-year-old let me crazy-mama hug him after church. I've been gone for two days, and he spent last night with a friend. Right there in the youth group hallway, he leaned in and let me keep hugging, and smiled like I am the silliest, best goofy mom he's ever known.

To touch someone can communicate a million things, but with my children, I have always wanted my touch to say to them, *I am madly in love with you. My love is unconditional. You will never outgrow your mama's love.* Through the years, I believe my touch has come to communicate even more things…

> *You are home.*
> *You are safe.*
> *You are accepted.*
> *You are welcomed.*
> *You are celebrated.*

To never stop touching your child means that you are respectful and discerning through the years. When my children were little, they sat in my lap. I carried them on my hip, held their sticky hands, and rocked those wiggly pumpkins to sleep every night. I would gather them on the sofa to read books, always touching a foot or an arm, making sure each one was close. We snuggled as often and as close as we could get. But I do have one child I've always had to go and get. Three would run to me, but that one would stand back. I decided that I would not let his hesitancy keep him away. He needed the touch of his mama, so I would extend my hug a little farther or leave the three to go and get him. I think somewhere inside he needed to know he was worth the extra effort. Today he's the cutie-pie, taller-than-me 17-year-old who still asks if I'm going to tuck him in.

As the children have grown, our touch has changed. Maybe they wanted to hold my hand on the sofa, but one day that wasn't cool walking into school. Today our touch is more mature and grown up, but I never want them to forget what if feels like to be hugged and kissed by their mama. So I don't stop. And they play along. And the message goes into their hearts...*I am loved*.

When I was a single mom and our world was insecure, I tried to lean into them with even more consistent touch and affection. Mandatory Uno games on top of my bed before bedtime. Movie nights with the five of us together on a pallet on the floor. Closer seemed to make us feel safer. Touch seemed to say to them, *We're going to be okay, I promise.*

Deciding to never stop touching them has become the thread woven through the tapestry of my mothering. Every area of our relationship is embroidered with the threads of affection. This strong thread that communicated love has taken the pieces of our differences, sewn us together, and made our family quilt strong, warm, and beautiful.

Reaching Their Hearts

Maybe sometime long ago, touching your child just slipped away. I believe moms have been given the power to restore affection. Reintroduce your touch as soon as you can. A loving hug. The stroke of their hair. A pat on the arm. Let them remember with the simple gesture of your touch that they are loved, they are yours, and the bond will never be broken.

Never stop touching them. The gift of your enduring affection will become one of the greatest gifts you ever give to their souls.

Kids Need Their Mom...

To Hang Hearts of Love over Their Lives

Today is Valentine's Day, and today my tradition continues. I'm hanging construction-paper mobiles in the kitchen before the kids get home from school.

Several years ago, on one of my single-mom Valentine's Days, I had baked a heart-shaped cake for dessert but wanted to do something else to make the house feel special. Store-bought cards were just too expensive so I found our stack of construction paper, picked out all the pink, red, and white ones, and then sat down to make cards instead. After cutting hearts in lots of shapes and sizes, I somehow ended up with heart mobiles instead of cards.

At the top of each mobile, I wrote that child's name. Then I taped a piece of yarn and attached another heart. On the next heart, I wrote something I admired about that child. Then more yarn and another heart until I had these long, dangling, multicolored, multishaped heart mobiles for each one of the children. I hung them from the ceiling in the kitchen. They looked pretty, but I had no idea how much they would come to mean.

That afternoon, the kids ran in from school, shocked for a moment by a kitchen of hearts and yarn. Turns out they loved standing there and reading their mobiles. I don't know, maybe I wrote things I had meant to say but had forgotten to say. Or maybe they were things I had told them hundreds of times, now written in marker and hanging for everyone to see. But whatever it was, all strung together like that, each child seemed to beam over how wonderful and unique their set of words was. The hearts were such a hit, we let the mobiles hang for a week.

On Valentine's Day the next year, one of the children asked, "Are we going to have heart mobiles hanging up after school today?" Honestly, after a year had gone by, I had already forgotten about the mobiles, but after carpool I sat down and crafted new strings of hearts with that year's words of affirmation. The children came home that day and again seemed to love reading their words over and over.

Later that afternoon, the boys brought some friends into the kitchen to get a snack. The guys were looking at all the hanging hearts, and I heard one of my boys say, "Yeah, it's our tradition. Mom does that for us every year on Valentine's." Who knew two years was a tradition? But now, many years later, it is. I think this morning they've probably forgotten they will come home to hanging hearts, but every year, it still seems to bless them so much. And every year, I look forward to watching them read about all the joy they bring to this world.

> Every day I wake up believing in and pulling for them.

What I've realized is that I can recognize the special things about each one of my children, but they really, really need to hear me say them. Or see those things on display. Or overhear me brag about them to a friend. In these years I am trying to be aware of the little and big things they bring to this life and make sure to highlight their best things.

Seems like my more instantaneous thought is usually about something they have just done wrong or something they could improve if they tried a different way. The hanging hearts that first Valentine's have taught me that they thirst for recognition. They need me to say, "Hey, I see that little sprout of great character inside of you." Not only do they need me to see what is great inside of them, they need their mom to call it out. "Honey, you should do that more! You really shine when you do that."

Finding the good and highlighting it is sometimes a little work. If your child is going through a trying time, it can also be a bit of a stretch! Some years you've got to work to find the good things buried deep inside that heart. But if there was ever anybody in this world who could find what is good and valuable and noble inside of your child, it's you. I am so grateful that I see my children through my mother eyes. Sure, I'm pretty clear about where they need to improve, but every day I wake up believing in and pulling for them.

What a gift we will give to our kids if, in our own unique ways, we hang hearts of affection and love over their lives:

You are such a good friend to our pets. They all love you very much.
You have an amazing eye for detail. How do you draw graffiti like that?
No one can beat a video game faster than you. I have the coolest kid.
Show me that kick-flip again. You went so fast, I almost missed it.
Your friends really seem to listen to you. I think you are a leader to them.
When you smile, everybody in the room smiles back.

I love all the free social media, and as newfangled as it still feels to some of us, the reality is that we are never going back. Social media is the means by which our kids will communicate for years to come. You and I can become the high-tech early-adapters and use all the new technology to pour blessings into their tender hearts.

It might not be a pink construction paper heart, but a message given in love does the same thing no matter the means. Social media lets you give a shout-out to your pumpkin, randomly, whenever it comes to you. I text my kid at school to say, *I'm praying you rock your test.* I text my daughter who lives hours away several times a day to let her know she'll never be far from my heart. Sometimes I post a message to her Facebook page that only she will understand. Or send a HeyTell. Our family stays connected when we're apart with Twitter and check-ins and Skype.

Reaching Their Hearts

Here's to all the moms with eyes to see the hidden qualities ready to blossom inside of their children. And here's to using paper and yarn, new apps and camera phones, and whatever comes next to hang hearts of encouragement over their lives.

4

Kids Need Their Mom...

To Watch Them Go Out of Sight

Long before the days of airport security, there was a bit on an old television show that went something like this:

> A guy takes his girlfriend to the airport to catch her flight and then returns home to his roommate. Roommate says to the guy, "You drove her all the way to the airport? Wow, she could have just taken a cab. When you got to the airport, did you drop her at the curb or park and walk her in?"
>
> "I walked her in."
>
> "Did you say good-bye at the ticket counter or go with her to her gate?"
>
> "I went to her gate."
>
> "Did you leave when she boarded the plane or stay to watch her plane take off?"
>
> "I watched her take off."
>
> The bewildered roommate gives his summation: "Man, you're in love."

I probably remembered those sitcom lines because that's what my dad did for us. He stayed to watch us go out of sight. Always. Years ago when nonflyers could still walk you to your gate at the airport, I'd board my plane to somewhere, look out of my window, and see my daddy standing inside the terminal waving at my plane. I can't imagine how he could see my face pressed to my window waving back, but it always seemed as though he could. The psychology of these things is something I don't understand. All I know is that his staying until I was gone gave me comfort. I felt loved.

So as a mom, I watch until my kids go out of sight. These days the airports are different, but I stay until I can't see them anymore. As long as I can squint them into sight, I stand there just to be a comfort. When my kids are flying, Scott and I watch them get through security, and then we go over to a hallway where we can watch them walk the long corridor to their gate. As they come around the corner, I'm standing there waving and smiling and mouthing *I love you* one more time. And here is what is amazing to me—they walk down the concourse toward their gate, take a dozen steps, and then turn around and wave again. A dozen more steps, another turn and wave. I've had them turn around five or six times until neither one of us could see the other anymore. Sappy, I guess, but it means something to all of us.

> My kid always knows that I've stayed.

It's the same for camp, retreats, and sports. Our family doesn't do the drop and run. We put the camper on the bus and stand on the curb. Most of the time I can't even tell where my kid is sitting, and when there are a lot of buses, I may forget exactly which one they're on. But I stay. And wave. And smile at all of them as they pull away. It's so interesting, even if I can't see them, my kid always knows that I've stayed.

When it's crazy cold in winter, I just kiss my family out the door, but when there's a little warmth, I follow the whole brood to the car in the morning. Through lots of kisses and several trips back into the house for forgotten things, I stand outside in my big, snuggly robe and wait until they leave. Most of the time I walk to the end of the driveway waving while they back out, and if it's really warm, I offer a little first-thing, morning entertainment with my version of jig dancing while they pull away. I have to believe that even the sleepy teenagers are smiling on the inside because their mama is dancing in her bathrobe in the driveway. I feel that somehow, my watching them go out of sight gives them the same thing it gave to me. Comfort.

One Friday afternoon, I was out of town so Scott took then 12-year-old AnnaGrace to the church to ride the bus for fall retreat. He laughed because on the drive there she gave him the talk. The young parenting instructor said, "You do know that you can't just leave after I get on the bus. You have to stay until the buses pull away and we've driven out of sight." Evidently Scott said, "You've got it, baby," and he stood there with three or four other parents while a few hundred kids headed to the beach for camp.

Reaching Their Hearts

So next time they have to leave, stay. Stay until you can't see them anymore, and wait like you mean it. No words need be spoken. Your smile and your wave will tell them everything your heart holds.

5

Kids Need Their Mom...

To Keep a Date Night with Dad

Around our house, Wednesday night means date night. My husband and I wake up Wednesday mornings and whisper to each other, "Date night. Woohoo." We send little encouraging texts to each other during the day—something like, "Yuck, I know that was hard, but hey, we still have DATE NIGHT!" When you live with four kids and their friends and run a business and travel like a tour guide in between, those two little hours together in the middle of the week have become one of the sweetest gifts we give to our marriage.

I hope this doesn't sound awful to you, but on Wednesday nights we take the kids to youth group at church, dropping them off at 6:15 (about 15 minutes early) and picking them up around 8:10 (about 10 minutes late), and then for one whole hour and 55 minutes, we have date night. I realize that a lot of grown-ups go to church on Wednesday night, and I am a huge fan of Wednesday night church, small groups, and Bible studies. It's just that in our season of life, I am usually in church somewhere in this country all weekend long. If Scott and I are going to have a date night, for now it's Wednesday night. I think the whole idea of date night is that after your relationship with God, you keep a commitment to build your relationship with your spouse.

On Wednesday night, we gleefully shoo the kids from the car and race to a restaurant around the corner from the church. The whole idea about hurrying is that we'll have more time to sit and linger later. I don't think either of us care where we go or what we eat—there is just such a peaceful-ness about walking into even a coffee shop, hand-in-hand, ordering together and then sitting to talk about anything, or nothing. I usually glance at my watch a few times to say, *Wow, we're doing great on time.* We've gotten into the habit of ordering small and sharing something. Taking our time. Rushing to get there so that we don't have to rush through the most important part—being alone.

> Our commitment to date night seems to give them a confidence about us.

We have learned the hard lesson of trying to have date night at home. It sounds good and really inexpensive. It's just that it doesn't work for us. A few times we thought we could go home and sit on the back porch, have some cheese and crackers, and watch the sun set over our patchy grass. Maybe some people can do that. But then there's the mail. And the dryer beeps. And the neighbor who stops by to visit. And before you know it, date night at home isn't a bit peaceful, and time has run out, and not one lingering moment was had. So we gave up on the homestyle date night, but maybe it would still work for you.

The reason I think your kids need you to keep a date night is that it models the order of your priorities for them. Most Wednesday nights, one of the kids will ask, "Where are you going for date night?" They know we're only running around the corner to sit and talk and enjoy each other, but our commitment to date night seems to give them a confidence about us. We're talking. Laughing. Working through hard things. We like being together just as much as we like being with them. It matters that they see us committed to that time alone.

I do have to warn you, date night is the first thing you will try to give up when you're stressed. Every week, I can think of how many productive things I could do with two quiet hours at home. There are closets to rearrange. Writing deadlines to meet. I could even get my grocery shopping done in that amount of time. But date night has to have a protective, non-negotiable, permanent barricade around it. Everybody else can come up with a million ways to fill your time, but this one thing matters too much. The world can't have it. Keep your date night safe so that your soul can be filled.

Before I close this chapter, I want to give a shout-out to my single moms. I was you for almost eight years. The purpose of date night in my marriage is soul nourishment. As a single mom, I needed the same thing…it's just that date night was more often a few hours with my girlfriend or neighbor. A couple of hours to sit together with a friend. Talk through my crazy life.

Listen to her. Share an uninterrupted meal. And in my single-mom years, that usually happened on a day or an evening when my kids were visiting their dad. For several years, on my Thursday nights free, another single mom would have me over to her house. We'd eat something simple and sit on the back porch. Amazing how her dust and beeping dryer never bothered me. It was a time to catch my breath, talk about my heart, and let the sweetness of friendship refresh my soul. Single moms need date nights too.

On Wednesday nights, after just our little time alone, Scott and I are usually ready to see the kids, hear about what happened at church, and reenter their worlds of homework, sports, and friends. And what is so cool is that just our few hours renews our joy. We enjoy the kids more that night because we have had the time to look at each other and affirm each other.

Reaching Their Hearts

Kids need their mom to keep a date night because even small things like two unrushed hours restore the weary and renew the heart. After date night, I know I'm a better mom. I've been heard and understood. I've been seen and encouraged. I've rested for a moment and collected my thoughts and my intentions. And I can give to my children from what has been given to me.

Keep a date night, my friend. Your soul and your marriage and your children will thank you.

6

Kids Need Their Mom...

To Make Them Sit Around the Table...and Linger

My kids like to eat standing up. Arrghh. I can't bear to watch anybody eat standing up. Must be the Southern girl in me, but it just seems people ought to stop for a minute, sit down, and eat properly. So I make my family sit down together when we eat. What I am *not* saying is that I always prepare a fabulous meal, set the table with proper dishes and linens, light all the candles, cue the music, and then call my family to the table in my lilting "mother knows best" voice. Sometimes that actually does happen, but mostly our meals are a random mix of anything goes.

I just happen to be married to a really great cook (I have acquired 20 of the happiest, yummiest pounds to prove it), so many nights he'll say there's something he wants to make. Sometimes I come through with an old-time mama dinner like meatloaf and mashed potatoes. At least once a week, we pick up some kind of pasta from around the corner, and just as often we meet at our local Greek restaurant between sport practices and meetings.

At this place in my mothering, I have died to all the dreamy visions of how I wanted my family to share dinner. Now, the only thing I care about is that we are together, sitting down, and looking at each other most of the nights each week. A few nights ago was our family Valentine's dinner. I tried to pull together something special, but by the time we coordinated our schedules, we could not get everyone around the table until 8:30 p.m. That's late eating for us! But I am convinced that being together matters more than the time that you eat. So we waited. And I made the starving eat some cheese and crackers. When the last stinky soccer boy got home and the whole family sat around the table, it was such a sweet relief to be together. They all ate like Olympic athletes, but even better, the conversation was rich and fun. We talked for hours and finally had to make the break for baths and homework.

Scott and I have decided we actually get the best "face time" with the kids when we go out to eat. When we really want an extra dose of hearing them and looking at them, we meet at the little cheap café down the block. What we've realized is that as much as we like cooking at home, we're distracted by the oven and the stirring and the setting of the table. The kids have their homework in front of them, the computer is popping up messages—it's just too much. When we sit around that table at the café, those nights are worth the cost because no one is preparing anything.

> We are… communicating to them in the simplest way, this time is valuable, but looking at you is one of the best things I've done all day.

No one has to let the dog out. We just look at each other and let the day and our hearts unfold.

I think it's a pretty popular thing to do, but we started "highs and lows" many years ago. It's a great way to open up conversation with your kids or to hear something you may not have known otherwise. Each person says their high point and their low point for the day. It's okay not to always have a high or a low, and every once in a while a child will have three highs or four lows. The idea is to talk about that person for just a minute, hearing what stood out for them. Scott and I never get left out. The kids always remember, "Okay, mom, highs and lows?"

I've really tried not to be an uptight rule keeper about eating together, but I think my kids know that it is a nonnegotiable family value. If we have takeout or drive-thru, that's fine—let's just sit together to eat. Sunday night is our "crazy" night. It took me several years to embrace this one, but on Sunday nights, we all sit in front of the television to eat dinner and watch *The Amazing Race*. Everybody's yelling, *Hurry up! It's gonna start.* And now with DVR, we don't begin watching until the last straggler makes his plate and gets seated on the sofa. I know it's kind of goofy, but it's our family and we like our silly traditions.

I'm hoping that around the table we are teaching the children the fine art of lingering. Just for that time not being in a hurry. Communicating to them in the simplest way, this time is valuable, but looking at you is one of the best things I've done all day. Pretty early, we started a corrective phrase that goes like this: "We are encouragers." You know it's going to happen that one child gripes at another or mumbles something sarcastic under their breath. A long time ago I began to look at the negative one and strongly say, "Hey, we are encouragers in this family. That's not allowed here." It's a family byline now. We are encouragers.

Reaching Their Hearts

I encourage you to have your family sit around the table and linger as often as you can. Keep this time upbeat and supportive. Everybody in this world needs a safe place to come home to. A place where they can have a meal and say the truth of their heart. A place where people are pulling for them. A fan club. Your table is the perfect place for this to happen.

Kids Need Their Mom...

To Let Her Yes Be Yes and Her No Be No

Jesus said it clearly, "All you need to say is simply 'Yes' or 'No'" (Matthew 5:37).

What Jesus meant was, be clear about your intention and don't say anything you don't mean. Let your word be your promise. And don't embellish your words to try to manipulate your own way. Plainly put, let your yes be yes and your no be no. Jesus was talking to His disciples and all who would decide to follow Him. But this principle is so strong, I think it's our responsibility as the mom to highlight the instruction with our own lives.

I don't know of another era or generation where it would be more important for us to model this character trait for our children. Our kids need a mom who will think through her response and then give a yes or no the child can depend on. Sadly, almost no one else is doing that. Every area of social media is about an illusion, an impression, or a spin. Many of our leaders say one thing to one audience and then take a different slant with the next. It is currently cool to be wish-washy, keep your options open, and go with the flow. What may be hip is not what our kids need from a mom. They need us to make grace-filled decisions, mean what we say, and then keep our word.

My kids can think of a thousand things for me to do. I mean it. When they were little, I called them the "can I haves." I loved going to the grocery store without the "can I haves." But now that they are older, they have become

Can I go?
Can they come?
Can you take me?

Can you come and get me?

Can you give me?

Can you help me?

Can you buy me?

Can you stand on your head and sing, 'cause I'm bored?

Left to their own little natures, these people who are my children would come unglued with their overwhelming desires! They can think of so many things. I've learned that the easiest thing to say is no, because that immediately gets me off the hook. *No. Nope. Not gonna happen. Nada.* But no is not always the correct response.

> I have built a history of trying to keep my word with my children, so even if they are disappointed, they can trust that I will still make good on the new plan.

As their mom, I have learned to respond to the kids the way I would like someone to respond to me. I try to take enough time to think about my answer, and then I respond to them with a decision I believe I can keep. A long time ago, someone told me to say yes every time I can, so I've tried to do that. Every time I can say yes, I do. When I have to say no, I usually give my no accompanied by a quick explanation. I like rational explanations, so that's what I try to give. I can't ever remember saying, "Because I said so," but there have been a few times I've said, "It's not appropriate for you to know the details, so you'll just have to trust me—my answer is no."

Sometimes I've had to return to my child and say, "Yesterday I promised we would buy new cleats this afternoon, but the schedule has changed, so now it looks like we will have to go on Saturday." I have built a history of trying to keep my word with my children, so even if they are disappointed, they can trust that I will still make good on the new plan.

Kids need their mom to keep her word because several things happen when we do. First, we are training them to be like Jesus. Second, we are building their sense of security, teaching them how to trust in someone who is trustworthy. And third, we are building inside of them the character of a future great leader, parent, and spouse.

Reaching Their Hearts

Maybe you haven't done a great job with letting your yes be yes and your no be no. Here's what I love about following Jesus…it's never too late with Him. This very day you can choose to become a mom who thinks, commits, and keeps her word. How cool would it be for your children to watch you become that kind of mom right before their very eyes!

Kids Need Their Mom...

To Be Delayed, Rerouted, and Canceled with Poise

I was speaking in Orlando for a weekend, and it seemed like just the right time to take my 13-year-old daughter, AnnaGrace, with me. Our tickets were booked well in advance. The day of departure finally came. We arrived at the airport that Friday morning with bags, an itinerary, and lots of enthusiasm. We were happy as clams, just the two of us off for a mother–daughter adventure.

We were unable to check in at the kiosk, so we had to move over to the counter. That is always a bad sign, but I was hopeful, assuming it just meant our flights were delayed.

"I'm sorry, ma'am. It appears we have your reservations for this flight, but you have not been ticketed," the lady behind the ticket counter said.

So I calmly and methodically started, "Gosh, I am a platinum flyer with you guys, and I've never heard of such a thing. Your website says my daughter and I are on this flight, and your computer system sent me emails yesterday reminding me to check in. I'm confused."

"Well, ma'am, you do not have tickets. To fly to Orlando today is going to cost you $2200," she said with a straight face.

I had been completely calm and reasonable right up until that moment. The $2200 part was so shocking that the inside of me instantly wanted to cry or scream, but with my last modicum of poise, I said, "I'm so sorry, but I cannot pay $2200 for tickets I have already paid for. If I thought I owed you $2200, I would pay it, but I am sure that cannot be right. Is there a supervisor here?"

She left to talk to the manager. I was sure he would get this straightened out. Had to be some kind of cyber misunderstanding. The straight-faced agent returned. "He said he would waive the $300 reticket fee, so that'll be $1900."

Time was going by; we needed to be at our gate; and the whole time, AnnaGrace was standing right beside me, witnessing this huge unfolding travel catastrophe. I could feel my heart pounding as I said to the agent, "I have to fly today. I am speaking tonight. But I cannot possibly give you $1900. Can I see the supervisor?"

In the next 45 minutes, I felt completely unheard and not believed. The agents yelled at each other, slammed phones, and snapped at the crew to get our bags off the plane. The supervisor made calls and typed furiously. The plane took off without us, and right then and there, my poise was gone. I physically felt it leave me. We were both standing there dumbfounded. I couldn't believe this was happening to me and my babygirl on our trip for two. Looking back, I think that is the moment the Holy Spirit took over. Something inside of me was determined to keep this huge mess from owning my countenance. Even though I could feel myself trembling, I kept standing there as though I had just been appointed the leader of this uncooperative team, reassuring my airline people that we were going to figure this out and it was all going to be okay.

> Our kids need us to teach them what to do when we have been misunderstood and misrepresented.

Finally, the supervisor looked up and said, "I've found the mistake. It's in our system. The agent who reserved your flights did not process the ticketing. This has been our fault. I'm so sorry. You will be delayed, but we'll get you there on the next possible plane."

I turned to AnnaGrace and she whispered, "Good job, mom."

Honestly, I had been so focused on getting to my speaking engagement, I had totally forgotten that she was taking this all in. Then she began to give me the play-by-play recap. "When that lady said $2200, I knew you were frustrated, but you never lost it. Anybody else would have been screaming and swearing and throwing things. I'm so glad you're different."

Oh my goodness, I was glad I didn't lose it too. I'm not really a "lose it" kind of person, but that situation could have done it. Teaching Anna-Grace how a godly woman should react to aggravation was more important than getting us to Florida that morning. She needed her mom to handle an annoying inconvenience with poise.

Our kids need us to teach them what to do when we have been misunderstood and misrepresented. They need to see us respond to difficult people and difficult circumstances with an older sister kind of perspective. Not letting ourselves be pulled into the fray of hurtful words and explosive emotions. We can teach them how to stand up for themselves with grace instead of defensiveness. You don't have to cower and back down to be godly, but you do have to intentionally choose your words, your attitude, and your position. A godly woman acts differently when situations blow up and decides to respond with maturity instead of selfishness.

Reaching Their Hearts

Now here's the thing: We cannot give what we do not possess. Each one of us must keep pursuing a spiritual and emotional maturity so that when it's needed, we have something to give. Maybe you are reading this today and thinking to yourself, *Oh my goodness, I have already blown it so many times in front of my kids.* They've seen your short fuse. They've heard your immature rants when something goes wrong. Well, here's the very great news. You can change.

Believe me, in this world you will have another opportunity! When the next tense situation comes up, wouldn't it be great for them to see you handle that one with poise? Wouldn't it feel good to respond from a place of composure instead of anger? Everybody in this world is ready to teach our kids how to have a tantrum. How to be furious and rage when you are misunderstood. But who is going to teach them about poise under pressure if not us?

The toughest thing about teaching this principle is that the instruction happens in the heat of frustration. I'm praying that you and I can respond from a spiritual and emotional maturity, so that our hearts will be prepared when the inevitable difficulties come. Our kids need a mom like that.

9

Kids Need Their Mom...

To Make Them Wait to Take a Bite

My boys. My starving, "Come on, mom, we're dying" boys. They will fill their plates, run to the table, and just start eating. 'Course the girls will do that too without a mama there to say, "Hey, everybody, wait!"

I want them to wait until we all are served. Wait until the whole family is sitting down. Wait until the prayer has been said. Just hold on one second and use your manners and stare down at your food and wait. It's agony-inducing for them. But it's the right thing for us to do. Kids need their mom to teach them a few manners. Painful as it is for all of us, somebody has to civilize the rascals, and the job falls mostly to you and me.

> We're training our kids from their earliest ages to be respectful of the people in our family and the people we will meet in this world.

When we're walking into a restaurant or store, I stop at the door until one of my sons opens it. Sometimes he stops too and we just stand there, but I always out-wait him. He knows what to do, but he is a kid in training and he forgets. Open the door for your mama and hold it until everyone is through. I think they like to test me sometimes to see if the rule still holds. But I am a determined woman, and yes, the rule always holds. Our sons should hold the doors for us, their sisters, their grandmothers, and all the people coming into the restaurant behind us. Besides, what else do they have to do? Hurry to the table only to sit and wait until everyone has been served?

They need to know which fork to use, how to write a thank-you note, and how to look people in the eye while giving a well-intentioned handshake.

They need to give up their seat for anyone from an older generation. And they should keep an eye out for people who need help and assistance. Having manners comes down to just being polite. We're training our kids from their earliest ages to be respectful of the people in our family and the people we will meet in this world.

When the kids were younger, we'd be on our way to someone's house or an event and I'd keep them in the car with a minisermon that went like this:

> *When we go inside, I want everybody to look at people and say hello. I want you to speak up with a clear voice when someone speaks to you. No mumbling. Give a good strong thank you, yes ma'am, and no sir. Let's go get 'em!*

There is no telling how many times I have given that talk. Hundreds. Thousands. But I'm pretty happy to say that most of the time, as teenagers and young adults, they know how to look at people and respond to them. Of course, we do have a 15-year-old in the house, and he is in the season of grunting, so it's still a struggle for that one. But even for the grunter, I know he knows what to do. Word on the street is that he grunts less when he's not at home. Hard for me to believe, though.

I have tried not to be the uptight, rule-keeping, manner police with knuckle slapping and evil glares. Hopefully I am more of a regulatory agency, overseeing the little mannerless people who live with me until they mostly get it right. Reminding them for about 20 years until, I hope, they will finally remember for themselves.

You know how it goes with your kids and manners. At home you can begin to believe they're going to grow up and live like barbarians. Then they spend the night with a friend, and the mom tells you that you have such a well-mannered child. It's downright shocking that they can absorb what you tell them, practice the right thing at a friend's house, and then whine like a baby at home because you make them wait to eat. And use a napkin. And not talk with their mouth full. And other annoying stuff like that. What I think that means is that we're doing good. It's going inside of them…slowly.

I do have to confess that this manner mama had to apologize to her son William just last week. The entire two years that boy wore braces, I fussed at him to chew with his mouth closed. We decided it was the braces, and so when they came off, I told him I was giving him three weeks to change his ways. *No more chewing with your mouth open. It's disgusting and you know better.* In the meantime, I took William to see an allergist. We sat with the doctor in his office to review the numerous things William was allergic to. The doctor said, "Mama, I can just look at him and see allergy all over him. Look at the way he's breathing through his mouth."

And it hit me—the poor child can't breathe through his nose.

I said to the doctor, "I think I'm going to have to apologize to William in front of you. In the name of good manners, I have griped at him for at least three years about chewing with his mouth open. William, I am so sorry. I didn't know."

The doctor said, "Mama, the boy would choke if he chewed with his mouth closed. He can't breathe any other way."

I was humbled. And I learned something. My boy had not been intentionally disobeying. He had no idea why he couldn't make himself do what I'd asked.

Reaching Their Hearts

And so, word to the manner mamas, let's train our kids to be polite and to respect others with our actions. Let's teach them to see the world around them and how they can interact with graciousness. And what if, every once in a while, we let them off the hook. And we don't scold them for missing one door. Or reprimand them every time they sneak a bite when they thought we weren't looking.

Kids need their moms to teach them manners. And give them grace. And say they're sorry for being too hard. And all-in-all, remember that their hearts matter more than the right fork.

But getting the fork right is good too!

10

Kids Need Their Mom...

To Take Christmas to People Who Have Nothing

My husband says that when he was a little boy his mom would put him in the car with a basket of food or a bag of clothes and then drive him across town. Wherever they stopped, she would have him get out of the car and carry in whatever she had brought to the family they were visiting. He never had to say a word, just be polite. His mama did all the talking, and Scott just carried things in, stood, and listened. He says he can't count the number of trips he took with her or the number of places they went. "Anywhere she heard there was a need," he says. But the lessons of those trips are the lessons that shaped his huge heart of compassion.

Scott's mom believes that no matter how much you have, there is always something to share. Even for our family, she'll stop by the house with a bag of homegrown tomatoes or a bouquet of fresh flowers from her yard. We came home the other day to a box of hot doughnuts on the back steps. The kids hopped out of the car and instantly knew, "Nana's been here!" But I also know that we were just one of her many stops. She probably dropped off a few tomatoes for a widow down the street or took flowers to someone she just met in her neighborhood. My mother-in-law has a heart of gold, and she passed that to my husband. She taught him how to care about everybody, especially the poor, uneducated, and sick.

When the children and I married Scott about three years ago, he had already been taking care of several needy families in town. I had no idea while we were dating because he never said a thing. For years, he had been quietly taking holiday meals, gifts, and back-to-school supplies to several families who were surviving on next to nothing. The first Thanksgiving after we were married, he went to the grocery store, bought meals for several families, delivered them, and forgot to tell me until later.

"You did what?" I couldn't believe he forgot to mention this huge detail to me. So he told me what he'd been doing for years. And I told him, "I want in on that! And I want my kids to do what your mom taught you."

So the week before Christmas came, and I got to work. Scott bought his regular carts of food, and I found out that he also buys toiletry items, detergent, soap, and things like that. I loved adding to the joy by baking some cakes and cookies, and buying and wrapping individual gifts for each person in the families. The night we packed up our car was such a blast. I think we may have even driven two cars. We loaded up all the kids and told them what we were going to do. "We're going to visit some families who don't have very much and give them some things to make their holiday brighter." The kids wanted to go, but none of us had any idea how addictive the giving would be.

> The seed of giving was planted in their hearts. I prayed it would become their passion.

That night we pulled up to a tiny home that Scott had visited for years. There were no signs of holiday there. No Christmas tree. No strings of lights. Not a wreath on the door. It took all six of us several trips to unload the food and gifts we had brought. The elderly grandmother cried and cried. Her sons wiped tears from their eyes. Her grandchildren stood in the kitchen awestruck. They kept telling our children thank you with each new box that was stacked on the table. I watched my kids take in the sweetness of giving. I could see how humbled they were. I could see the obvious registering in their hearts: *we have so much, they have so little.*

Before we left, Scott asked if we could pray for them. My kids needed to stand in that dimly lit kitchen holding hands with people they had never met, smelling the smells of nothing on the stove, feeling the cold of not enough heat, and bowing their heads to pray for God's provision for that family. I know the family was grateful we came, but I was so incredibly grateful that my children were standing inside a lesson that would shape them for a lifetime. As we left that first home, the grandmother hugged all the children, spoke blessings over them, and told us all to come back anytime. The seed of giving was planted in their hearts. I prayed it would become their passion.

We made a few more stops that night and all the holidays since, but this past Christmas we had a different version of the lesson. This last December, one of the families knew we were coming, but when we arrived, the house was dark. And it wasn't just dark. It was spooky dark. The kids and I thought nobody was home, but Scott had a different idea. He knocked and knocked on the door, and finally the back door creaked open about a foot wide. The man Scott knew was there, along with several other people. It was the situation Scott had feared. They where home, but using drugs, too embarrassed or too strung out to answer the door.

So there we were, a family of six bringing Christmas to a crack house. I didn't have a clue what to do. Do you give Christmas to a whole houseful of law-breaking drug addicts? Well, apparently you do. Scott told the kids to unload the sleigh, and there they went, sliding one box and bag at a time through the barely open back door. Scott did all the talking to the person inside the house. Nobody else said a word. Honestly, that stop went pretty quick. I was ready to get into our car, lock the doors, and get out of there. When we were well on our way, I looked over at Scott like, *Oh, my, what just happened?* Loud enough for everybody to hear, he humbly offered, "Everybody needs Christmas."

No one in our car needed another sermon about what just happened. God had preached a sermon that would shape our souls. Everybody needs Christmas. Everybody needs the love of Christ. Everybody needs somebody to be Jesus to them.

Reaching Their Hearts

We have to teach our children that no matter how much we have, there is always something we can share.

Kids Need Their Mom...

To Miss a Few
Things They Do Wrong

Grayson was about three years old. His big sister was seven, and his baby brother was a newborn. I was a frazzled mama, trying to do everything right. We had been at my parents' house visiting for a few days. One particular day, it seemed that all I did was redirect the kids, tell them no, take things away from them. I employed all the usual tactics. Time out. Counting to three. And especially, a lot of talking. I stayed on top of them like a hawk that day, trying desperately to protect my parents' house, and more importantly, protect my great mom reputation. They were not going to do one thing wrong, at least not on my watch.

By the end of that night, I had put the three of them in bed and tiptoed back downstairs to sit with my parents for a while. I was pooped. The kids had worn me out, and I had worn me out. It's exhausting to be the little world police. My dad didn't give me a talk that night. He didn't even elaborate. He didn't have to. All he did was look at me with the most sympathetic eyes and offer this statement that from that day forward changed me as a mom. "Angela, you don't have to see everything they do wrong."

Daddy's words landed exactly as they should have. Grace for the perfectionist. Humanity for supermom. Freedom from the striving. Relief for the children. What daddy meant was, I know you are going to see everything they do, but you don't have to call them on every single thing. It's exasperating to all of you. Release some of this determination to live with perfect people and just let them be children. Very good children who, by the way, will need a Savior just like you did.

Daddy was right. Great moms see most everything but learn to use discernment about when to address a behavior and when to miss it, on purpose. I am so very glad he spoke to me that night. A few more years could have gone by, and I might have just exploded from all the uptight, all right, building inside of me. For that matter, the children may have exploded from all the pressure. And when children explode from the pressure they've felt, it can sometimes look like anger, rebellion, emotional distance, and hurtful behaviors. But for the grace of God and my dad's intervention, it could have been us. And I could have stayed in the sin of exasperating my children.

> To miss a few things our children do wrong does not mean to turn a blind eye to bad behavior or attitudes.

Last spring I traveled to South Africa, and my parents came to our home to help Scott with the children. After I returned and had settled back in at home, my mom said she needed to talk to me about something. She was distressed about William's room. "It's awful. He just throws his clothes down, and you can't even walk in there for the cleats, soccer balls, and gym bags. You have just got to do something with him. He knows better than that. And it smells bad."

She was right. William needs to do better. The other kids have neat and tidy teenage rooms. They take care of their things, and they can usually find what they need. William is a disaster. You always know where he has been because there is a little trail of stuff. As I am typing this very moment, his room is above me and to this day about the same, except we have opened the windows to work on the smell. He is my messy boy.

It's interesting to me that my mom had forgotten. She had forgotten that many years ago, she had chosen not to see.

I said to her, "I agree. William's room is awful, and it's bothered me for years. I've had so many talks with him and fussed at him and made rules for him and punished him. But then one day it hit me. There was a woman I am very familiar with who did the same thing when she was younger. ME! Mom, do you remember how awful my room was? I would run in from school, step out of my clothes, and leave them on the floor while I hurried to the next activity or homework. There was clutter and girlie junk everywhere. Do you remember what you did for about four years? You closed the door."

I could see the light come on. She did remember.

I continued, "William is a really great boy. He makes straight *A*'s. He loves God with all of his heart. He is the busiest person in the family, running from one soccer practice to the next. Because his heart is so good and all his other choices are so right, I've decided just to close his door too."

To miss a few things our children do wrong does not mean to turn a blind eye to bad behavior or attitudes. It means that we don't keep pointing out every flaw, annoying our children to an extreme. I have encountered some moms who just will not give it a rest. *Nag, nag, nag. Gripe, gripe. Correct. Complain.* It seems to never stop. And the poor children—anyone can look in their eyes and see the defeat of having a mom who never misses anything. I know a particular young woman with an exasperating mom. She just moved away to college. She loves her mom, but guess what? That daughter comes home only when the school closes the dorm. And who could blame her? It must be so peaceful not to live with the constant criticism and nitpicking.

Reaching Their Hearts

Kids need their mom to miss a few things they do wrong, not to let them off the hook but so that we can exhibit the character of Christ. To allow more room for grace. To keep a balanced perspective about what matters most. To be a peacemaker instead of a perfectionist.

I'm so thankful God used my dad to stop me in my tracks that day. May He keep us all from becoming demanding and hard to please. And oh, how I pray that our kids will want to come home from college to moms who overlook the little things and love them like crazy.

Kids Need Their Mom...

To Put Down the Phone

I have a 15-year-old son who plays soccer. Several years ago, I realized that even though he runs onto the field focused on the game, warms up joking around with his buddies, and plays his little heart out like he doesn't even know I'm there, that kid can tell you where I was sitting in the bleachers, who I was sitting beside, and especially if I was talking on my cell phone. Even texting. It's amazing what they are taking in, even if you think they're not looking.

And here is the saddest part. When my son sees me talking on the phone in the stands, it sends a message to him. *I'm just here because I have to be. I'm not really interested in what's going on out there. The person I'm talking to is more important than your silly game.* Of course that message is completely wrong. It is not the reflection of my heart at all. But nevertheless, it's the message my phone distraction sends to my kids. On the soccer field. In the car. In the kitchen.

Of course, there are times I have to answer the phone. Anytime a child calls, I answer the phone. If my husband or parents call, I answer the phone. But after that, I have been spending my mom years learning phone boundaries. Sometimes the phone and the emails and the texts can wait. It can just all wait, especially if I'm supposed to be giving my attention to someone I really love a lot.

When the kids were little, they would be quietly playing in the next room. The phone would ring, and it seemed like a fine time to talk on the phone. The kids were occupied so what did it matter? But over and over again, when I would be on the phone, my kids would come and stand in front of me.

And crawl on me. And want things from me. I couldn't understand why they would always need me when I was talking on the phone.

Finally it hit me. They were in the other room going along perfectly fine, and then from somewhere close by, they heard my sweet voice. The one I use when I'm on the phone with a girlfriend. And they heard me laughing.

And they thought to themselves, *Oh, there's mama's sweet voice. I like it when she's using her sweet voice. I love it when she is laughing like that. I'm going to go to her. I want to be close to her. I want to sit with her. There is my sweet mama.* And they would come to find me because they loved that version of me.

> They needed me to react with happiness when I saw them, not shoosh them because something was more important.

Now that they are teenagers, not much has changed. They are fine if I take a call, but they'd much rather have my attention. I try to get off the phone as I'm driving up to the school for afternoon carpool, but sometimes that doesn't happen. When they get in the car, I can see the looks on their faces if I'm on a business call or talking to a friend. I feel their hearts disconnect as they sulky-sit quietly until I'm done. They just wanted me to look at them first thing. They needed me to react with happiness when I saw them, not shoosh them because something was more important. Truth is, when I have been on the phone as they jumped to the car, I have forfeited one of the best mom moments of the day.

Some of the phone boundaries I am trying to hold firm are:

- No phone calls or texting at meals. Not for me and not for anybody else.

- I don't get on the phone before my kids leave for school.

- I try to wrap up my business day, emails, calls, and texts as I'm turning into the carpool lane for afternoon pickup. I may cut it close, but I try to say good-bye before I pull up.

- I make phone appointments during the day or after bedtime to talk to girlfriends for those fun, chatty, catchup calls.

The time with our children is fleeting. My 20-year-old daughter lives four hours away, and some days I wish I'd learned about putting the phone down sooner. How many times did she see the back of my head, my hand to my ear, instead of looking into the eyes of her mom? How many times did I turn her away instead of picking her up?

I can't go back and redo, but I certainly have tried to change. After we get home from school, my phone is turned to vibrate and left in my purse. Also, I finally learned how to disconnect the automatic email on my phone so that it's not beeping and vibrating all the time. If I want email, I can manually retrieve it, but no more constant beeping. At night, if the kids are busy, I'll occasionally check my phone, but pretty much by five, I'm done. Whatever it is, it can wait until tomorrow. My cell phone is the direct line to me. My general rule is to ask people to call my cell phone if they need to reach me. I'll answer if I can. They can leave a message, and I'll call back. My family and friends also know to call the house if it's urgent, and somebody there will help find me.

Too many of us are controlled by the whim and wiz of technology. It's a beautiful tool, but we can't let it own us. Or divide us from our children. Or demand that we respond when better judgment says *not now*.

Reaching Their Hearts

What if all the moms just put their phones down, especially during those critical times of the day, the beginning and the end? What if you were fully present for the hellos and good-byes? And what if your family decided no talking on the phone in the car and no phones present at meals? Our kids need us to put down the phone and ask them to do the same. Someone has to teach them priorities and manners, and I'm pretty sure those lessons begin with us.

Hey, all you soccer moms and dance moms and hockey moms: they may act like they don't care, but they see you over there on the phone. One day we'll wish we had a game to go to, but all we'll have is too much time to sit around and talk on the phone.

The phone can wait. Your child, being heard by you, matters more.

Kids Need Their Mom...

To Learn Their Unique Love Language

M y four children, two girls and two boys, are alike in many ways. Chocolate chip cookies are a home run with the whole crew. They can usually agree on the kind of music they want to listen to. The beach is their favorite vacation destination. They like to eat outside and travel to new places, and I can always count on my kids for funny stories. Each one of them can tell a great funny story.

But oh my goodness, for all their similarities, they are each one so incredibly different. Each child is in process on their own life journey, still becoming who they are going to be, but already we have one artist, one engineer type, a closet writer, and an actress. Our four fill the entire spectrum—neat and messy, loud and quiet, ambitious and hesitant, sporty and not-so-much. We have a little bit of everything in our house.

One part of our children's differences has to do with their love languages. In his 30 years of experience, marriage counselor Gary Chapman observed that everyone he had ever counseled had a "love language." He says that a love language is "a primary way of expressing and interpreting love."* His work has helped to heal marriages around the world, but it turns out that primary love languages begin to take shape at an early age in our children. His books *The Five Love Languages of Children* and *The Five Love Languages of Teenagers* can be powerful resources to us as moms.

The whole idea is that we would learn the love language of each one of

---

* Gary Chapman, www.5lovelanguages.com/learn-the-languages/the-five-love-languages, accessed March 2011. For more information go to www.5lovelanguages.com.

our children. Understanding what speaks love to them. Realizing what connects with their heart. The love languages that Dr. Chapman lists are these:

- *Words of affirmation*—For this child, words speak louder than actions.
- *Quality time*—Undivided attention is what this child craves.
- *Receiving gifts*—A well-chosen gift (not materialism) means something to this one.
- *Acts of service*—This child hears love when you do something to help them.
- *Physical Touch*—Hugs, holding hands, and snuggling say "I love you" to this one.

Not surprisingly, I have one physical-touch, one quality-time, one receiving-gifts, and one acts-of-service kid. Not to say they don't appreciate or feel loved in other ways, but it has become obvious through the years which language speaks loudest to each child.

> It might speak big love to one child to kick the soccer ball with him, and to another one, snuggling on the sofa is the shout.

As moms, it is so valuable for us to take the time to learn our children. To know as much as we can about who they are, what they like, and what they want to become. But one of the most special things we can do is to learn, as early as possible, their primary love language. I hug all my kids all the time. (Physical touch is my primary love language. Many times you give love in the ways you like to receive love.) But if I only hug the child whose primary language is quality time, I have not spoken their language. My love for them has not been communicated as "loudly" as I wanted it to be.

It might help you to go through Dr. Chapman's books, first assessing your own love language. How do you express and receive love? Before I took some of his assessments online, I was sure I had to be all five types! A full-fledged love bucket who needed everything. It turns out that I have an order. I enjoy all of the languages, but physical touch from my family speaks to me the most.

When you begin to understand how you feel loved, you build a good foundation for learning the love language of your child. Then you can better direct your love communication. It might speak big love to one child to kick the soccer ball with him, and to another one, snuggling on the sofa is the shout. When one of my children is going through something difficult, I always try to think of ways to make them feel safe and cared for. And I want to communicate my care through *their* love language, not mine!

With all the great technology, it's so much easier to for us to love well. You can Skype with the child who lives far away but still needs some of your undivided attention.

You can text your words of affirmation the very minute they pop into your head.

Just yesterday, I went by the high school and put a notebook in my older son's car because his doors have keyless entry. It meant the world to my boy with the acts-of-service love language.

Physical touch is still physical touch, and thankfully, I don't think any technology will ever replace a good old hug. But the child who needs physical touch may need a plane ticket home for a little hug refueling.

One of the best things my child can say to me is "Awww mom, you know me so well." Truth is, I want to know them, and as they grow and change, I want to know the new, more grown-up version of them. I don't know what Dr. Chapman says about love languages that change, but I do know if that happens, as their mom, I'd like to be one of the first to observe and embrace the change.

Reaching Their Hearts

Kids with moms who speak their love language feel known. It's got to be a pretty special feeling to be a kid in this hard world and then to go home to the mom who not only loves you but is actively trying to know you. When you rank the gifts we can give to our kids, I think this one would rank pretty high.

To Occasionally Be a Supermom

Before you throw this book across the room, hear me out. If there ever was a defender of the normal, average, run-of-the-mill kind of mom, it would be me. Most every single day, I am just a regular mom who is doing a pretty good job, always wishing I were a little better at a few more things. There is no supermom cape hanging in my closet. And if I had one, I'm sure it would be wadded up at the bottom of the laundry basket, waiting for a load of colors to wash with it.

I realize there are probably some slacker moms out there, but honestly, I don't know any of them. Most every mom I know is doing the very best she can, given her circumstances, kids, and resources. For goodness' sake, our kids are fed, clothed, housed, and given medicine when they are sick. We are getting a lot of things right! Maybe we get a few things wrong every now and then, like punishing the wrong child while the other one hides in his room snickering. And then there are the moments when we just drop the ball. Like the other night,

> Every kid deserves to feel like they are worth the extra effort.

it was 7 p.m., and I had absolutely, positively forgotten to think about making dinner. The kids were looking at me from across their homework like *What has this world come to?* You already know what I said to them when I realized what time it was: "Put on your shoes. We're going out."

Most days as a mom are about managing the regular and the routine with an occasional catastrophe. I think if you can do that showered and wearing clean clothes, somebody should give you a gold star! But I also feel that, every once in a while, maybe not even once a year, but sometimes, our kids need us to pull a supermom caper. To me that means occasionally doing something a little over the top that makes them feel special and loved.

In my house, I've pulled a few supermom stunts to make sure one of my children received a few hours of lavish love. I think every kid deserves to feel like they are worth the extra effort sometimes.

One birthday comes to mind. I can't remember exactly what year, maybe it was Grayson's twelfth, but for some reason, it wasn't working out to have a traditional time to celebrate. With schedules and commitments, he wasn't going to be home, and there wasn't even a good time to just have cake and ice cream. But it was my boy's birthday! I remember thinking, *There has to be something I can do to make this day a little more special.* Then it hit me, a surprise breakfast birthday party before school! I called the moms in our neighborhood to ask if their boys could come in their pajamas about 5 a.m. They thought I was crazy but, go figure, all the boys were free at that hour and would be there.

I got up about an hour before the party and decorated with streamers and balloons, and started frying bacon and mixing the waffle batter. When the eight neighbor boys arrived, I had them all go upstairs and wake Grayson. He was so happy about his birthday surprise, and it's one of our best party memories. The party wasn't expensive. It just took a little supermom ingenuity to pull it off. And to have Grayson come to me later and say, "Wow, mom, that was so fun" was worth any sleep I lost and the extra effort it took. He felt special. I'm so glad we didn't let his birthday pass that year.

Maybe being an occasional supermom means hosting the soccer families at your house for a covered-dish dinner. Or letting eight preteen girls camp out in your living room so they can giggle all night, leave snack bowls everywhere, and then act grumpy in the morning because no one slept more than an hour.

Maybe being supermom means agreeing to be the team mom, just one season, not forever.

I feel like supermom when I get a completely homemade dinner on the table. I confess that those meals are kind of rare these days, but occasionally, I still try to pull one off. I want my family to know I love them enough to spend those hours in the kitchen.

I don't think being the occasional supermom has very much to do with finances. Sure, sometimes it costs to feed a few more kids or do a little extra, but what I mean by this is the idea of giving of yourself and your heart. It doesn't cost any more money for me to make homemade yeast rolls. It just takes a lot more time. So I do it once a year. The super-duper, incredibly yummy, Thanksgiving yeast rolls that take me all day to make. They're a once-a-year supermom gift to my family just to bless them.

Reaching Their Hearts

What would it mean for you to occasionally be a supermom for your kids? And by occasional, I mean occasional. Infrequent. Not expected. Not a bar you set and keep raising with each new idea. Something that says to your child, you are worth a few extra hours or a little inconvenience. You are even worth my getting up early or the whole house having to listen to silly girls all night. How would it make your children feel if every once in a while you just wowed them with your big heart? I think they'd feel special and significant. Every kid in this world needs to know somebody would do something special just for them. And it's especially important for them to receive that kind of attention from their mom.

Just a note to the women who want to be supermoms every day. Take it from the fried and crispy woman I have been, you may be successful for a season, but in the end, trying to be supermom every day will flat kill you. Give it up this moment and run as fast as you can toward being a regular, doing-the-best-she-can mom. Your kids and your mental health will thank you.

So let's all agree to go for the occasional, random-enough-that-it-remains-special act of supermom love.

15

Kids Need Their Mom...

To Turn Their Beds Down at Night

I never saw her do it, but when I was a little girl, my mama would go to each of our rooms sometime before bedtime. In the winter, she would turn on our electric blankets. In the summer, she would turn down our beds. My uncle lived with us for a couple of years, and I remember walking past his room one night and looking in. Mama had turned down his bed too. For some reason it stuck with me, *Oh, she does that for everybody.*

Turning on our electric blankets or turning down the bed was a small gesture, but even as a child, it left such a huge coziness inside of me. Mama never made a big deal about it. She never stood up in her housecoat and announced to all of us, "I'm going to turn your beds down now." It just happened. Like the kindness elf had gone room to room. When bedtime came, I'd snuggle down under that warm electric blanket and fall sweetly asleep wrapped up in love. Amazing how the little things stay with you. And how they still speak to me as I remember my mom's selfless love and kindness to us.

As mom to my four, the bedtime tradition continues, though not with the same consistency. My mom was home every day and every night. She was an exceptional homemaker who set the bar very high for her daughter who didn't quite inherit the full spectrum of her homemaker genes. Some of them transferred, thank goodness, so I've tried to keep the same tenderness in our home that my mom established in hers, practicing the little things she did that made our home so comfortable and loving. The smocking and French hand sewing, well, I gave up on some things like that. Ripping out yet another crooked seam is exhausting. My time is better spent with words.

So every time I can, sometime before the kids go up to bed, I make a stop in their rooms. What kid, or teenager for that matter, wants to walk into a dark room at bedtime? Nobody. So I turn on their bedside lamp, turn down the covers, or turn on those toasty blankets. Like my mama, I try to make this round in secret. No proclamations. No fanfare. And maybe my mom used to do this—I've never asked her—but as I walk through their room, touching their things, I pray for them. Sweet sleep. A rested body. Strong minds. To feel loved in our home no matter what they may be facing.

> I want to bless them with soothing gestures. *You are home now. Here is the place of calm in your crazy, chaotic day.*

At night, in the rest of the house, I make my rounds to turn on the little lamps. Light the candles. Build a fire in the winter. Put on some music that is peaceful. One night classical. Another night Sinatra. Tiny, tiny things that create an atmosphere of warmth for them. I want home to feel and smell and sound calm to them. I have the great, great honor of setting the tone of our home, and so I have chosen rest and refreshment as a few of our themes. I want to bless them with soothing gestures. *You are home now. Here is the place of calm in your crazy, chaotic day.*

I have a friend who warms the bathtime towels in the dryer to wrap around the kids before pajamas. Can you imagine how cozy that feels? And how a gesture like that, in a most unspoken way, communicates kindness and love? Another friend waits at the afternoon bus stop with bottles of cold water and an afternoon snack for her kids as they come home from school. A cool drink from your thoughtful mom. How great is that?

Trust me, I'm not running a day spa here in Pamperville, but oh my goodness, if there were ever a group of people I would want to bless with small gestures of kindness, it would be these people. My family. My children. What will it matter if I have been thoughtful to guests who stay in our home but haven't felt my kids were special enough for this kind of warm affection?

The place they live should be sweetest, safest place on earth. I am more and more convinced that our homes do not have to be fancy to communicate secure love, but there must be an atmosphere of goodness and hospitality to give them the soul foundation of being welcomed and glad in their own home.

As moms, we have the privilege of adding the little touches of tenderness to their lives. Things we can do to create a haven of rest and peacefulness. This is not a wait-on-them-hand-and-foot mentality. These are simple deeds done solely for the purpose of blessing. To bless the ones we have been entrusted to care for. To communicate unconditional acceptance. To say to them in the smallest ways, *you are a really big deal to me.*

Reaching Their Hearts

I love to turn their beds down in secret for a couple of reasons. It's an unspoken gesture at the end of their day that communicates one last love impression before they fall asleep. I'm pretty sure that they barely notice that I do it anymore, but one day, when they are grown, I believe that warm memory will give them comfort. And when they are old enough to process it, they'll know even more fully the depth of love simple touches added to their growing up.

Maybe tonight, before the kids get to sleep, you can slip into their rooms to turn on their lights and turn down their beds. And tonight, they'll end their day snuggled by simple kindness from their mother's love.

16

Kids Need Their Mom...

To Ride a Roller Coaster...
for the First Time

Thunder Mountain. My stomach hurt just to think about it. There in front of me stood my greatest amusement park fear. Roller coasters. You see, I have always been a waiter. And a holder. All my life. Really. Not kidding. No exceptions. I have always waited for everyone else to ride the fun rides while I sat on a park bench to hold all their stuff until they came back. Sometimes I sat for hours when the lines were long and the youth group wanted to run back and ride again. Did you hear that? I have spent countless hours in this short lifetime sitting on park benches all over this country waiting for my friends while they did something fun. Do you know what kept me on the bench? Fear. Paralyzing. Stomach sickening. Fear.

I come from a family of fear. But it's not really our fault. My sister drowned when I was young, and my parents couldn't bear the thought of anything happening to another child, so we played it safe. Extremely safe. Better not to risk anything than to experience another tragic loss. No one could bear to think of it.

The old joke about my grandfather Cecil is that "he quit school because they had recess." Translation: he didn't play. But who could blame him, my grandfather watching his mother burn to death in their house when he was six years old. I imagine that something inside his soul died that day too, and he never played again. I come from a long line of workers. People of great integrity who live for God and pay their bills, but we don't play. The truth is, the loss that my family has known scared all of us. We're too afraid to play.

So, I have spent all of my life being safe. Which is just fine and dandy when you are one person and it affects no one else. And when your friends roll their eyes at your insecurity and then hand you their cotton candy because they're not afraid to play. It's just fine to miss every adventurous, silly thing when it's just you. But it's not just me anymore. I have become five people.

When the kids were smaller, I did try to address some of my fears. Growing up, my family stopped anything that had to do with water after my sister drowned, but I didn't think I could do that to my children. I had them all in swim lessons at six months old. And I kept them in swim lessons until they could not only "roll over and save their own lives" but swim like fish. Then I watched them like a hawk mama. Standing by the pool pacing whenever we would go. Never letting them go into the ocean deeper than their waist. For years, I'd take my kids to the beach and stand all day in the water holding their hands, monitoring every single move. Still desperately afraid but resolved not to pass on the fullness of my "not playing" heritage.

> As I am able, I'm going to try not to pass the irrational on to my children.

I had never in my life put on water skis or been pulled on a raft behind a boat. At least not until the day the kids begged me to ride with them. On the lake with our friends, I was just fine in my role as boat mama and chief sandwich maker. I didn't have any intention of conquering any fears that day. But the kids were relentless. And even more, I realized I didn't want to keep passing down the legacy of choosing stifling fear over low-risk fun. With our life jackets tightly buckled, I jumped into the lake with my kids for one of the few times in my life. I hoisted myself and two children onto a raft and then held onto us all for dear life as the long rope from the boat began to pull us across the top of the water. I was completely and totally petrified. But the more time went by, and the more my children laughed, the more my fear subsided. Do you know what I learned that day? Playing is fun.

Several years later in DisneyWorld, I was standing with then 13-year-old William. Unfortunately, he had been the unwilling recipient of many of my fears. He too had become a watcher and a waiter. Roller coasters and fast rides weren't his thing. As a little boy, he was content to sit in my lap and watch everyone else, just like his mama. By 13, I decided that I had been partly to blame for planting the seeds of fear inside of him. It was truly okay if he really did not want to go, but I felt I had to at least try to help him not spend the rest of his life like me. Waiting and holding.

We were with a big gang of family and friends standing at the base of Thunder Mountain. Everyone was racing to get in line as fast as they could. But William held back. He had never ridden a roller coaster. I could see the anxiety in his eyes. He wanted to go, but he was just so afraid. I pulled him over to the side and said, "If I go, will you ride with me?" Somehow in a flurry of fast talking, I persuaded him to get in line with me. The whole winding walk up to the top, I knew he wanted to leave, and I kept asking myself, *What in the world have you done? You don't ride roller coasters!*

But there we were, two of the biggest chickens on the planet, locked into a roller coaster that was getting ready to move. It was too late. I thought to myself, *Even if I faint, I probably won't die, so I guess it's going to be okay.* Well, as you can probably guess, William and I had the best ride of our lives. The train pulled back into the station, and we were both laughing, half-crying, and high-fiving. I told William, "That was my first time to ride a roller coaster." He said to me, "Let's do it again!" And we did. Straight off and back in line. I think we rode Thunder Mountain five times that day.

I'm so very sorry that irrational fear kept me waiting on too many park benches. I've missed a lot of good fun and laughter. But as I am able, I'm going to try not to pass the irrational on to my children.

Reaching Their Hearts

Kids need their moms to confront some of their fears. Realize where they came from. And then intentionally break the chain.

Maybe your kid needs you to ride a roller coaster for the very first time too.

17

Kids Need Their Mom...

To Talk to Them like They Are Fascinating

Confession. I can glaze over. Yep, just completely lose track of what is being said right in front of me, go somewhere else in my mind like *Oh my goodness, I'm ready to take these shoes off,* and before I realize what's happened, I have missed at least two or three sentences, maybe more, from the person who is talking. I don't mean to do it because I place such a high value on listening, but the awful truth is I catch myself in this quandary all the time, wondering what was just said and whether it was important enough to ask them to go back and start over. Glazing over must be the unavoidable outcome when a person has taken in more than their weary head can hold. I bet you've done the same thing.

But you know what happens with our children? We have grown accustomed to their voices. Their little babbling in the background becomes the soundtrack for our days. Even with a house full of teenagers who are acquiring grown-up voices, sometimes their words blur together in my head, and their familiar sounds become my own personal, wacky elevator music. I love the sound of being in my house. Even when it's crazy, it soothes me. But sometimes in the familiar, I realize that I have not paid attention to my family. I was just going along enjoying the family hum.

A few years ago, a line from a lecture challenged my glaze-over tendency. Something the speaker said landed firmly in my heart and I decided, *I want to talk to my kids like they are fascinating.* It's not really a stretch to make that kind of decision because I am fascinated by their thoughts and ideas. It's just that weariness and workload have many times crept into my head and distracted me from the very people I really want to hear and understand.

When the kids were little, talking to them like they were fascinating meant stopping what I was doing, many times kneeling down or stooping down to look them in the eyes or hold them in my lap until they finished the story they wanted to tell me. They also wanted me to look at their papers carefully, noticing the small details and then hanging their art on the refrigerator. They wanted me to care about all of their stuff.

Years ago, I didn't know what to do with all of their stuff. You know what I mean by stuff—all the things they get that really matter to them at the time. Certificates, art folders, report cards, special awards, and the not-so-special awards they just have to save anyway. We call all those things keepsakes, and all the kids have keepsake boxes. Lots of them. I started the keepsake accumulation with one plastic, stackable tub for each child with their name labeled on the outside. For each of the four children, I kept tubs in a handy closet and just sorted the "keepsakes" as they came in until that tub was full. The attic is now stacked with lines of keepsake boxes, but we're not done yet. To this day, one of my teenage children will hand me some little piece of paper and say, "It's a keepsake," which means that paper, or piece of string, or whatever needs to go in their special box. I don't think we can ever move from this house because there are too many boxes in the attic to bring down the ladder.

> There are nights when I intentionally try to stay up until they are talking...the deep, reflective things that seem to come later, when we're all in our pajamas.

Now that my kids are older, talking to them like they are fascinating means I can keep working on dinner while they are talking to me, but my mind has to be engaged. Good grief, they are so smart, and they catch every time I have missed something important they wanted to say. These days, my best stay-engaged method is to ask them questions. If one of them says, "Mom, I missed two questions on my history test," then I am learning to follow with, "What do you think happened with those two?" And even a follow-up to that like, "How could you study differently next time so that those details stick with you?" Honestly, the dinner prep conversation is easy. It's usually about schoolwork, schedules, things they'd like to do, or people in their lives.

Now that I have teenagers, our best fascinating conversation happens late at night, and oh my goodness, is that hard for me! I am an early-to-bed, early-to-rise kind of mom. And they are night owls, every single one of them. A girlfriend warned me several years ago, "You'll have to stay up with your teenagers until almost midnight if you want to know what's in their hearts." I remember thinking to myself, *Not mine. We'll get all our talking done during the day.* But she was right! They open up at night. Late at night.

Even though most nights I can barely keep my eyes open past ten, there are nights when I intentionally try to stay up until they are talking. I'm not looking for the sleepover silly talk, but the deep, reflective things that seem to come later, when we're all in our pajamas. The walls are down. Everyone feels safe. And the fascinating talk flows easily. As their moms, kids need us to talk to them like they are fascinating, but sometimes that means looking for the environment and circumstances that open their hearts for sharing.

Reaching Their Hearts

I want my children to know in their deepest places, *Mom loves talking to me. She is interested in me. She cares about my interests. She thinks I'm funny. I make her laugh. She believes in me and always sees the best in me.* When we talk to our children at every age like they are fascinating, we are transferring to them a deep security. It's a gift of love that can never be taken from them. To know that you are adored by your mom is a treasure that gives you strength for a lifetime.

Kids Need Their Mom...

To Treat Their Friends like Family

O kay babydoll…"
     I've probably given this drill a hundred times to all my kids' friends.
"Here are the rules for our house:

- You are welcome here. Truly. Tonight you are at home with us, and we're so glad you're here.

- You are welcome to anything we have in our kitchen. Want a glass of juice? Just pour one for yourself. Cups are there.

- No one goes to bed hungry in our house. If you need a snack, it's yours.

- Need a bath towel? Check the bathroom cabinets.

- Make yourself at home here, sleep comfy, and stay as long as you can."

Maybe not the first meeting, but certainly by the second, I greet my kid's new friend with a hug and "mama love." My version of mama love might go a little like this:

> "Marco, where in the world have you been? I sure have missed seeing you around here. Get yourself over here and have dinner with us."
>
> "Oh, thanks, but I'm not that hungry," Grayson's friend said a few nights ago.
>
> "But you are a growing teenager. Just a little something? At least come and sit with us and tell us everything," I keep going.

"Okay, well, maybe I'll have some of those potatoes," Marco decided.

I don't hover or try to hang out with my kids' friends, but it does mean so much to the children to know their friends will be welcomed graciously. We want their friends to walk into our house and know that a whole family full of people is happy to see them or meet them for the very first time.

One of the best ways I have learned to treat their friends like family is to put them to work. Nothing big, but included. When I come home from the grocery store, I call every name in the house to go and bring in the groceries, even if they are all squirrely 12-year-old boys. If a friend is just standing around before we serve dinner, I hand them the placemats and get them setting the table. I send them to get firewood right along with my kids. I'm not looking for free labor. I just know how being included makes me feel.

If I am at a girlfriend's house, one of the sweetest things she can do is hand me a knife and put me to chopping. I'd much rather help than watch. Then I feel like we're on the same team. I'm contributing, and the sweet bond of connection happens so much faster in the sharing. Keeping a houseguest as an observer keeps them at a distance. I think it's the same for my kids' friends. In their most awkward growing-up years, it's a gift to their esteem and their sense of security to feel included instead of distant.

My children know that their friends are always welcome. And we mean it. They are welcome to spend the night. To stay for dinner. To come home with them from college. The kids usually remember to ask us first, but they know there won't be a penalty if they forget. The children also know that we are going to wrap our arms around their friends and be interested in who they are and what they are becoming. The other night around the dinner table, an international student was eating with us. Before our "highs and lows" time began, I heard one of the kids saying, "Get ready because you're going to have to say your highs and lows too." Sure enough, when our family was done, we turned to our new friend, who in his broken English told us his best and hardest parts of the day. I think the friend felt included, but even more, our children liked making him feel like family.

Sometimes I know we're going to have extra kids and I'm prepared, but

> My children know that their friends are always welcome.

sometimes it's a complete surprise. One day I was in a hurry and drove through the taco shop to bring home lunch. I pulled in the driveway to a yard full of boys and only one bag of eight tacos. Yikes! What I learned that day is that kids don't care what you serve them—it's how you do it. I ran into the kitchen and whipped up two boxes of cheap macaroni and cheese. Sliced three apples into a bowl. Made a couple of turkey sandwiches and cut them into quarters. Rummaged around for some cookies in the pantry and a few leftover chips and salsa. Put the whole smorgasbord on the kitchen counter and called them all in to eat. I was instantly a hero to my boys, "Wow, mom, this is the best lunch ever!" From that day on, I stopped worrying so much. Content didn't really matter. What mattered was sharing what we had with their friends.

Reaching Their Hearts

Making their friends feel like family is about opening our hearts and sharing what we have. It's the smile on our faces. The tone of our voices. The interest in our questions. The easy way we laugh. The "mama love" we give, even to someone who is almost a stranger.

We treat our kids' friends like family—first, because we have been invited into the family of God and the Bible instructs us to give what we have been given. Second, we welcome their friends like family because it makes our kids want to bring their friends home, and that's always where I want them to be. And third, we treat people like family in front of our children so they will learn. Oh, how I pray my children will make gracious, inviting homes of warmth where my grandchildren will live and grow.

I have one last thought. If we treat our kids' guests like family in order to show them a gracious love, what if every once in a while we treat our family like guests? Maybe every now and then we bring out all the "just for guests" goodies and gestures for our kids? And what if there is nothing attached to our giving? No special celebration. No big day. We just remember to treat them like guests occasionally to show them value and make a few memories and treat them to tastes of lavish love.

Kids Need Their Mom...

To Cheer Wildly from the Stands

Yesterday Grayson ran in his first track meet. He is a junior in high school and my second-born child. All the kids combined have participated in almost every sport available in our little world, and as their mama, I believe I have come to understand my role. I am supposed to pay the fees, keep their uniforms clean, get them to practice and games on time, pack a healthy snack for the player and the family spectators, fill the water bottles and remember the Gatorades, let the coach be the coach, let the referees call the penalties, clap politely for all the team, and most of the time, just try my best not to do anything that might cause embarrassment for my child. I'd say most of the time I do a pretty good job keeping to the sporty parent protocol.

But doggone it, sometimes I think it's okay for love and pride to kick in, and then a mom should be free to go with her heart. And for the record, nobody ought to judge a mama who cries over a soccer goal or yells a little too loudly for the stunning three-pointer or stands up and high-fives every person she can get to when her kid scores the winning point. At times like that, kids don't need a polite mom who is happy on the inside. When something big and wonderful happens on the field, kids need their mom to cheer wildly from the stands.

Take yesterday for instance. Grayson is our first family member to run track, and yesterday was the first track meet any of us had been to. Lacrosse we've done. As a matter of fact, cross country, baseball, softball, football, basketball, soccer, cheerleading—the kids have been sporty kids, trying and sometimes eliminating new sports all the time. But yesterday was our first time in the track-and-field bleachers. Grayson didn't really have any idea what to expect, and so he hadn't given us any expectations. We thought we were going to watch him and give him support, and truth be told, from the way he talked, we thought we'd be supporting him at the back of the pack.

During the track meet, Grayson ran his first 1600. For the rest of you moms like me, that's four times around the track. It's also about a mile. I know I sound smart, but until yesterday, I had no idea. I picked up the other kids at carpool, and we arrived at the high school where the meet was being held. Right off the bat I felt awful. Other moms had brought their kids bananas and water and refueling drinks. When will I ever learn? Always bring stuff if there is a sport involved. I had stopped to get an after-school snack for the other two kids, but it never occurred to me that my runner might need something too. Poor kid. Some mom somewhere should write a handbook and pass it around. I have all these children and I still don't know these things. Somebody please just let me know in advance!

Anyway, it turns out that a track meet is slow. Very slow. Kids were doing their homework. Moms where knitting. Small groups were forming all over the bleachers to stay warm and share food and just visit. About two hours into introducing myself to track moms and visiting about nothing, it was finally time for the 1600. I put on my distance glasses to zero in on my boy. He was down there somewhere with all the other blue shirts. The competitors lined up. The gun sounded and off they went. I finally spotted Grayson. He started in the middle of the pack, kind of like I'd expected, but by the second turn, he was passing people. And by the third turn, he was running in second place. I was shocked. And when the boy you expected to be at the back is running in second, a mom cannot keep sitting underneath her blanket in the bleachers.

I never had a conscious thought when my heart told my body what to do. All of a sudden, the blanket was off, my feet started moving, and as fast as I could get down there, I was standing at the fence by the time Grayson made the first lap past the stands. And you gotta know I was cheering and clapping and yelling with everything my full heart had to give. In just a minute, AnnaGrace was standing beside me as we yelled him around the next couple of turns. Holding onto second place, that kid just kept running like the wind. Another turn went by and Grayson's very cool, 15-year-old brother, William, couldn't help himself either. He got down to the fence, and we were all three cheering like mad when Grayson made his next lap in front of us.

Two more laps went by and a very tired Grayson was overtaken by a couple of runners at the finish line, but you've never seen a happier family. We were all so proud of his effort that we made our way down to where he was. As soon as Grayson saw us, we were pumping our hands in the air, whooping and hollering and running to hug him and relive that great run. He was smiling from ear to ear, my eyes were full of tears, and we all just laughed together over the complete and total fun of it all.

> I remembered that the one who mattered most to me just ran the race of his life. And his mom let her heart tell her how to respond.

When I got back to the stands, I realized that most of the other parents were still snug underneath their blankets. Still sitting like reserved spectators. Politely participating in a distracted sort of way. Returning to my seat, I felt a little sheepish at first until I remembered that the one who mattered most to me just ran the race of his life. And his mom let her heart tell her how to respond.

Reaching Their Hearts

No matter what they do—track and field, studying hard, loving their future spouse, working hard to support a family, serving God, growing in faith—no matter what and no matter where, I pray my kids know that their family, and especially this mom, will always be standing to cheer wildly.

Kids Need Their Mom...

To Give Grace-Filled Consequences

Consequences are one of the biggest things I despise about being a mom. Poopy diapers, not a big deal. All the laundry and dirt, I can take it. Schedules and food and school activities and homework, they don't get me down. But the consequences I have to give to my children, they make my stomach hurt.

First, I am not a confrontational person. Second, I like to avoid conflict every time I can. Third, I like giving happy, happy, joy, joy to my kids and not discipline and punishment. And fourth, administering the consequences is just plain hard. I don't want anyone else to do this for me because the discipline they need has to come from me. But most days I wish my kids would just be perfect kids who don't need any consequences so I could avoid this yucky part. All four of them have turned out to be sinners who need a Savior, just like their mom. And doling out consequences is a part of this journey called motherhood.

To give them grace-filled consequences means that you and I will have to be filled with a grace that guides our decisions and our words. If we are empty of grace, operating with frayed emotions and selfishness, then guess what our kids will get? Angry consequences. If you are an empty woman, you will discipline from your emptiness. That kind of discipline is many times too heavy-handed and too severe. Empty women very often give punishment that doesn't match the crime. Equally as damaging, an empty woman can also decide to do nothing because she is empty and tired and distracted, and the child, who needs grace-filled consequences, suffers from lack of discipline.

A grace-filled consequence is thoughtful and reasonable. Sometimes, grace-filled consequences pop right into my head, but other times, I'm not really sure what to do and so I take a day. During my single-mom years, discipline was especially tricky. I was so tired for most of those years that I had to make myself step up, do the hard things, and give and then enforce the discipline. Because I am nonconfrontational, my nature wanted to avoid hard things with the children, but my commitment to mother them well wouldn't let me off the hook.

> With each version of consequences, we have tried to take something awful and give moments of grace as God leads.

When the children were little, I remember hearing Dr. James Dobson say, "Mama, don't just shout an instruction to your kids. Get up, go across the room, and address the behavior." After the fourth child, I realized why Dr. Dobson had said that. When you are exhausted, it's so much easier to stay where you are and just bark at the kids. And the sound of your voice rarely accomplishes anything. Even when you turn up the volume and say the same thing over and over. It really takes a commitment to get up, go to the child, and either remove them from their misbehavior or look them in the eyes to give a consequence. Going to where my child was making a wrong choice usually gave them a few extra seconds to decide to obey, and it also gave me a few seconds to choose grace-filled words.

When they were little I tried to express my disappointment in their choices without attacking their character. Now that they are teenagers, I'm even more concerned about the spirit inside of them. As their moms, we have to be concerned about protecting their precious hearts even as we call them to improved behavior, express our disappointment in a choice, and administer discipline. Inside each one of our children is a beautiful creation, given right from the hand of God. We are called to guide and shape that soul for the glory of God. It is sin for us to break and wound the spirit of a child in the name of discipline.

This week, one of my children brought home a progress report with a bad grade. For another one of my children, that grade could have been their best work, but for this one, the grade was just pure laziness. We had talked about pulling the grade up a few weeks ago, so the progress report had to be addressed with a consequence. When I remarried, my husband and I decided he would guide and direct the children as their stepfather, but I would continue to be the giver of punishment. To give a grace-filled consequence to my son last week meant that our conversation began something like this:

> Hey, honey. I got the email about your algebra grade. I'm not quite sure how the smartest kid in the whole family can get a grade like that, but I think I have an idea. It seems like you have disconnected your focus from the class. Do you know that you are a brilliant kid on your way to becoming a brilliant man? You are such a fun person to have in this family, and I hate doing this, but part of my responsibility is to keep you on the path toward all God has called you to be. This grade is not a reflection of your ability so there is going to be a consequence until we see sustained improvement.

We talked for a while. He was embarrassed because he really is such a great kid. But great kids have to feel the strong walls of your protection around them just the same. I took his cell phone away, primarily because of its texting distraction. I didn't have to go overboard to communicate to this one. I hugged him. I kissed him all over his head. I spoke encouragement over him, but the consequences were firm and grace-filled.

At this point with my children, I think we've experienced a pretty full range of punishment for disobedience. When my oldest daughter was completely grounded for a month with no means of communication, I would let her friends come by occasionally. I called them the prison ministry and gave them a half-hour pass to visit the inmate in solitary confinement. With each version of consequences, we have tried to take something awful and give moments of grace as God leads.

Reaching Their Hearts

Our kids need strong discipline and punishment when their behavior dictates. But above all these consequences, they need a mom who is full of grace, able to be stern when stern is required, asking the God of grace how to care for the ones He has entrusted to her love.

Kids Need Their Mom...

To Be a Passionate, Alive, Spiritual Lover of God

My journey of motherhood has not been what I had hoped for. As a matter of fact, many of my mom years have been downright awful. I never intended to be a single mom for almost eight years. I had no plans to live in a broken home with broken kids and a broken heart. This was not what I had dreamed for them or for me. I've heard people say they live with no regrets. Not me. There are a million things I would do differently if I could. And especially when it comes to my children, oh my goodness, I would have changed so much of their story if I had been the writer.

After becoming divorced, I lived with an almost paralyzing shame. Embarrassment. Pain. Heartache. Some days, I'd just look into my children's innocent little eyes and run to my room crying. I wanted something more like a fairy tale for their sweet little lives. We have not lived a fairy tale, or anything close. But one day, somewhere in the healing, it came to me, *How now shall we live?* The power of God's faithfulness to us just overwhelmed me. Even though we were broken and even though I had been such a mess, the biggest question seemed to be, *How could a broken family live for the glory of God?*

I knew it was God prompting my heart. It was Him whispering, *I'm not afraid of your brokenness or your imperfection. I have always known you would need a Savior. Now live for the renown of your Savior. Even with your broken story and your broken kids, Angela, inside your house, in the privacy of your home, live for Me! In public, watch Me be the lifter of your head. Trust Me. Look to Me. Glorify Me in all you do.*

I remember finally understanding that if my brokenhearted kids needed anything, they needed me to be full of the presence and power of God. They needed me to love God and seek Him with all of my heart. They needed me to live a passionate, alive, awake, Christ-centered life. The best gift I could give to my broken family was to live everything I believed about God and pursue everything He has promised to do in my life.

> The sweetest thing we can do for them is to pursue spiritual maturity in every area of our lives.

What better way to teach my children about the healing power of Christ than to pursue His healing for my own soul? I can't imagine a better illustrated lesson than having your own mom transformed right in your very house. It seemed like they would learn to lay down their propensity toward bitterness if I would do that first. Like they would learn to choose laughter over misery if I would lead. Like they would learn to trust God if I showed them how myself.

I have found that my children mostly believe what I tell them. Especially when they see that I believe it first. When I told them God would take care of us, they believed me. When I told them we were safe at night because angels stood all around our house, they slept like babies. When I showed them that you don't have to have money or the things everyone else has to have a fun life, they followed.

Many nights in our single-mom years, we ended the day with all of us on my bed playing the card game Uno. I'd always say, "Just one hand," but we'd laugh so much, and being together was so sweet, we'd always end up with five or six rounds before bedtime. The kids didn't know we couldn't afford to rent movies or buy cable or do extra things. They followed the laughter and the joy. God did a work in my life to take what had been broken and sad, and transform me into a woman who yearned for joy.

As moms, we have the great privilege of leading our children toward God, and the most powerful tools we have are our own countenance, heart, and enthusiasm. The sweetest thing we can do for them is to pursue spiritual maturity in every area of our lives, allowing the Holy Spirit to change us. And I mean really and truly turn us from the moms we have been toward the moms we can be. They will be intimately acquainted with every tone and gesture that changes in us because we are maturing as followers of Jesus.

That's the kind of thing that will shape them for a lifetime. If we will grow up in Christ, I believe with all my heart, they will follow.

Reaching Their Hearts

Our kids need their moms to be passionate followers of Jesus Christ, no matter the circumstances that have come to us or the broken journey that has become our story. What if you decided today, "I want to know how kids turn out when they have lived every single day in the same house with a mom who is a passionate woman of God"? I have been challenged by the Word of God to live like that woman. I will never be perfect, but I am becoming more like Him because I have intentionally chosen to pursue a passionate walk with God. Exchanging my brokenness for His healing. Trading my grief for His joy.

With all my heart, I pray that growing in Christ, every single day, will keep changing me right before my children's eyes. May they remember their mom as always changing, ever improving, and forever seeking. I hope they are able to say, "Mom never leveled off with God. She kept running toward Him with abandon all the days of her life."

Kids Need Their Mom...

To Indulge Their Silly

I am not a silly person. I love funny and witty, but silly, I am not. Silly doesn't come naturally to me. I think I probably came into this world too serious and uptight, so sensible is usually my go-to response. Believe me, I have wanted to be silly because when I was little, my friends would act silly and I would smile politely but never could get there in my heart. Silly things aren't funny to me. Slapstick humor just doesn't translate for me. Cartoons. Goofy videos. I just don't get them. Then I had kids. And God, in His divine wisdom, decided to give the least silly woman on the planet four very silly-acting, goofball children.

Along with the not-silly component in my character came a strong avoidance for costumes. I don't do costumes. I have the cutest friend named Kim, and she is a grown-up costume lover. That woman makes silly look so fun. One day in the carpool line she came knocking on my car window dressed like a teenager from the fifties, complete with poodle skirt, ponytail, and rhinestone-studded cat-eye glasses. She was hooting and hollering, dancing around in that skirt, and I wished like anything that I was her. It was Fifties Day at the retirement home she owns, and my friend never misses an opportunity to lead with her silly.

So, because silly doesn't come naturally to me, and because there are bills to pay and grown-up troubles to worry about and college tuition to save for, I have to actively choose to indulge my silly children. It's amazing how the children you adore can soften the old serious nature if you'll let them. One of the main things I've had to do is reframe my judgment and embrace their creativity. I grew up in a house without silliness. Not only did we not do silly, we judged silly as a foolish waste of time. I'm realizing that a child's silliness is not foolish, it's just plain fun sometimes, and shame on me if I take that joy from their childhood.

My firstborn, Taylor, has been and still is our family's silly-time leader. If it is good, clean, silly fun, that girl has done it. Costumes, makeup sessions, food contests, and hours and hours of silly songs, silly dancing, and silly jokes. As her sensible mom, I have learned that one of the worst things I can do is to judge her silliness as a waste of time. Too many times, I have wounded her creativity just because I don't think the same way. I have learned that my kids need boundaries for their silliness—"You can use one bag of flour for your papier-mâché body-wrap experiment, but not all the flour in the pantry." Or, "You can use wash-out spray for purple streaks in your hair, but you cannot make permanent changes."

> Sometimes, in some situations, being silly is the best option. And a mom who wants to love her kids has to set aside her levelheadedness and choose silly.

Honestly, indulging their silly has been one of the best changes mothering has brought to my own character. I have learned to laugh over the things that bring them joy instead of just keeping to my own sense of humor. I am learning greater creativity through their eyes and ideas. I even wear a costume for our annual Hallelujah party, which is only because seeing me in a costume brings them such joy.

If you are a sensible, pragmatic mom, silly kids will try your patience and then they will teach you patience. A couple of nights ago, my son William was supposed to be on his way to bed. I wandered into the kitchen after I heard him still in there.

"Hey, baby, you are supposed to be on your way to bed," I responsibly offered.

"I am, mom, but I was just trying to find a good song to drink my water to," my goofball responded.

The practical mom had two options. Scold him for his foolishness. Or help him find a good song for nighttime water drinking. I decided to go for the song. Sometimes, in some situations, being silly is the best option. And a mom who wants to love her kids has to set aside her levelheadedness and choose silly.

Most of the time, we have to act orderly in our house to keep this big ship of schedules and people running. We have to get places on time, keep up with our possessions, take our assignments seriously, care about other people, and give ourselves over to study, improving, and the big challenges in this life. But oh, thank God, my kids are teaching me that every so often indulging their silliness is just plain fun. And it's good for their souls and mine. I am sure God knew what He was doing when He sent these kids to me. If ever a serious woman needed to lighten up, it was me.

I want to create a home where my children's personalities are embraced instead of constantly judged. I want them to know that silly people can be sensible when it's appropriate, and sensible people can learn to embrace silliness just for the sake of fun. I want my mothering to communicate to them, *You belong. You fit. You can be exactly who God made you to be, and our family is better because you are here.*

Reaching Their Hearts

I realize that some of you are like my friend Kim. She is a brilliant, degreed woman who owns her own company and yet leads her family with bursts of silly fun. I just want you to know, I applaud you. And I think your kids will become amazing people because they have lived with a woman who doesn't take herself too seriously. What a privilege to be raised in your home!

And for the rest of us who are still learning, let us press on toward embracing greater fun. Maybe tonight I'll declare "A silly hat is required for dinner," just to keep stretching myself and embrace the kind of fun they love.

Kids Need Their Mom...

To Have a Hallelujah Party

As a Christian mom, Halloween has always been the hardest day for me to figure out. Fresh out of seminary, I was full of facts and hundreds of reasons to ignore the day, so in my first years of mothering, that's what we did. I just acted like nothing was going on. Of course, as the kids grew older, that plan went out the window. As early as preschool, they knew something was up. And that something called Halloween seemed fun, even if it had a little scary attached to it.

For several years, we chose the alternative Halloween option among Christians, the ever popular Fall Festival, also known as the Trunk or Treat, Harvest Carnival, and so on. At least with a Fall Festival, the kids could dress up in a not-scary costume, and there was candy to be had and games to play, so for many years they were satisfied with whatever the church was doing that night.

But one day they realized that most of their friends didn't go to Fall Festival at Halloween. Their friends stayed home in their neighborhoods and went trick-or-treating door-to-door at dusk in costumes. And my kids thought that sounded way cooler, except their mom was stuck. Costumes. Trick-or-treating. Door-to-door. It felt like an outright celebration of Halloween to me. For years I had told the kids, "We are not going to celebrate evil." And my head just couldn't get there.

It finally hit me. My kids do not want to celebrate evil. Not one of them likes to be afraid or even watch scary movies. They don't want to exalt darkness or cast spells or buy into the hype about wickedness. They just want to have to have good, clean fun on Halloween. So what was a mama to do? Hallelujah, that's what.

Somehow I decided that the whole world might spend a day focused on darkness, but we certainly didn't have to. So our house went alternative. The first year I came up with this party I called "Hallelujah on the Driveway." I decided that our house was going to be a light in the dark on Halloween.

A couple of days before Hallelujah, I sent email invitations to all the neighbors and some friends from church. I told the kids they could invite anybody they wanted to. My friend Lisa and I spent one afternoon stringing up every line of white Christmas lights I had outside across the driveway. My dad brought a couple of fire pits over. We had white candles in lanterns everywhere and as many happy pumpkins as we could carve.

> Our little house was truly a light in the dark that night.

I made about five pots of taco soup and asked everybody to bring an appetizer or dessert to put on the table. I provided drinks, hot and cold, and everything you'd need to make s'mores or roast a hotdog. Everyone was invited to come in costume if they wanted, but no big deal either way. That first year, about 80 people showed up. No one had to do anything but enjoy one another, visit, and laugh. The kids went to trick-or-treat in big groups, stopping back by the house for another snack every so often. It was one of my all-time best ideas ever, and our little house was truly a light in the dark that night. We had a blast!

As you can imagine, Hallelujah on the Driveway has officially become a family tradition. I think this year will be our sixth annual. It's a little work for me and a little planning a few days in advance, but the payoff for my children has been huge. They get to have something cool and fun at our house. And it's the one time all year I tell them to invite everybody they can because taco soup goes a long way. My teenage kids work on their costumes for a few days. And for me, the sensible mom, it's the one day I wear a costume, just for them. I have actually been a cave woman several years in a row. Cave women don't have to style their hair. Just put a bone in it and you're good to go.

The Hallelujah has become our way of saying to the world, "We don't need dark and spooky to have fun. We'll take your day and trump your scary with light." What has been especially fun is that our friends love coming over, watching the kids, and sitting in lawn chairs by the fire. And our kids' friends love having a great alternative. I've also learned to lay down the judgment. Last year one of the middle-school girls came as a very well-costumed and made-up witch. I hate the idea of witches, but I love that girl, and I want to have her in my house with her pointy hat, learning a little about why we celebrate Hallelujah instead of Halloween.

I really think Hallelujah could sweep the nation. Families taking the day back. Reaching out to the neighbors. Keeping it simple. Loving their kids and their kids' friends. Laughing a lot. Roasting s'mores. How much sweeter does it get than that?

So maybe you're thinking, *I can do that.* Here's the easy taco soup recipe to get you started:

Taco Soup

2 16-ounce cans of kidney beans, undrained

2 16-ounce cans of corn, undrained

2 16-ounce cans of tomatoes, undrained

2 packages of taco seasoning

1 16-ounce can of tomato soup

1½ pounds of hamburger, browned with onions

Toppings

Tortilla chips

Sour cream

Shredded cheese

Chopped olives

Chopped jalapeno peppers

Combine all the ingredients in a large pot. Simmer as needed. Place a serving of tortilla chips in a bowl. Dish soup over the chips. Garnish with favorite toppings.

Reaching Their Hearts

Hallelujah instead of Halloween? Why should we even consider such a thing? Well, mainly because I think we're supposed to live the truth of the Scriptures every single day of the year.

You are the light of the world. A town built on a hill cannot be hidden. Neither do people light a lamp and put it under a bowl. *[Or hide themselves inside their houses or in the gym down at the church.]* Instead they put it on its stand, and it gives light to everyone in the house. In the same way, let your light shine before others, that they may see your good deeds and glorify your Father in heaven (Matthew 5:14-16, italics mine).

Kids Need Their Mom...

To Keep a Family Blog

W ell, I finally took the plunge. There is so much talk about blogging these days, so one night in a quiet hotel room, I decided to build a blog. It's not a public blog or a ministry blog. I do not want to increase the traffic to my site or sell any products because of my blog. My blog is meant for only six people to read—my family.

Unless something really crazy happens with the Internet, I think this blog idea is going to be around until the end of time. It turns out that anybody can have a free blog for as long as they'd like and for any old thing they want to blog about. Building a blog seemed like a great way for me to write my heart to my family. I can write to them as ideas come to me, wherever I may be, and they can access the blog from wherever they are, even from their cell phones.

> I think what matters more than anything is that you begin to get your words down for your family, especially for your children.

Blogging feels like I am writing a book of letters to my high-tech family in a format they are already familiar with. And with the push of a few buttons, my words are formatted beautifully, complete with pictures I've uploaded, organized, indexed, and filed for them for years to come. I love that each one of my family members can interact and comment and eventually, whenever they want, write posts to the blog themselves. By the time you read this, there may be hundreds of websites to help you begin blogging. I have chosen to use the tools provided on wordpress.com, but you can also begin a free blog at blogspot.com. Evidently, the very tech savvy can add all kinds of bells and whistles to their blogs. Mine is clean and simple. Easy to read and very easy for this mama to use.

I think what matters more than anything is that you begin to get your words down for your family, especially for your children and the children of all the generations who will follow. My blog to my family began with this first post:

> This blog is for my children. I love the four of you so very much. I am every day in awe of God's goodness to us. You are mine. And I am your mom.
>
> What matters most in this world is that I have loved you well. All our years together are going by too fast. Some days I'm not sure I have said everything I wanted to say. I don't know if I have given you all that God intended for me to give. So I am starting this blog just for you. I hope that in these words there will be wisdom, direction, laughter, and above all else...love. It is my greatest blessing to be your ma. I pray every day that God will make me better and teach me how to love you more.
>
> And so, on this very day, your mama's blog officially begins.

On the blog format I'm using, there is a section titled "About." I decided to retitle that section "A Few Things Every Kid Ought to Know About Their Ma." In that section, I am adding details and information about me. My parents have transferred this history to me, mostly by spoken word, and to tell the truth, sometimes I can't keep it straight in my head. Who was born where, died when, and all the details that make up our family tree.

As I have time, I am writing a little history about me for my children. I began with with the obvious, my birth, and slowly I'm adding the next stops on the timeline with stories and details I still remember. I wish I could get my parents to do the same thing. I'd love to have a blog from them with timelines, details, pictures, and especially their words of wisdom and the stories I never want to forget.

A few days ago, after a phone call with my dad, I ran to the blog to save his words for my children. Here is the entry I wrote to them:

A Phone Call with PaPa

Yesterday I was talking to PaPa on the phone. He said, "Angela,

I have been working on this thought, and I want to give it to you to use if you want to." I said I'd love to hear it. PaPa said, "What I've come up with is this:

The house that you are building is where you are going to live."

I told him that his observation was brilliant. And it is. So, from PaPa, to me, to you. I want you to remember that the house you are building with *your life* is where you are going to live. I want you to build strong minds, strong bodies, strong hearts, and a strong relationship with God.

Building your life means thinking about the kind of life you'd like to have one day and building toward that. If you build a shoddy house, you will live in a shoddy house. If you skip steps, you'll be living in a house that can fall on your head any minute. If you act lazy and pretend like you don't care about a house, then you'll probably end up living in a pup tent.

Get the idea? Build something strong and stable and good. Then you'll get to live in the house you have built and be proud of yourself and your accomplishment. And your family will be blessed by your strength. Then there won't be any time to look around at the houses everyone else has built and be jealous that they did something while you were doing nothing.

Reaching Their Hearts

Get the idea? If it needs to be said or saved or passed on, a family blog is such a beautiful way to give your heart to your children. They may not care that you start one this afternoon, but I do know this for sure, a family blog will become the treasure that helps shape their lives and the way they parent their children.

A blog for your children. I think this newfangled technology might be one of the coolest ways to say the things you have always meant to say. And it just might be the legacy you leave for generations.

Kids Need Their Mom...

To Become Physically and Emotionally Healthy

M idlife. Forty-eight years old. I am still shocked that it's happened to me so fast. Science says that my reproductive years are probably over. The scary stories about menopause and perimenopause seem to dominate most of my conversations with other women my age. And this morning, I woke up with my right arm aching, shoulder to thumb, just aching. What in the world is that? It's midafternoon and I just took some ibuprofen for an aching shoulder. Shoot.

It seems like each new season of motherhood has new physical and emotional challenges. As the mom, that means in each new place we have to stop, reevaluate, and do whatever it takes to become physically and emotionally healthy. Our kids deserve the best version of us we can muster. And truly, God deserves that too. We all have limitations that will not budge, but I think we are supposed to become the healthiest women we can, given our physical constitution and circumstances.

What that means for each one of us will be different. For the mom who is a diabetic, becoming healthy might mean managing her diabetes and keeping diligent watch over her foods, sugars, and exercise. For a mom suffering with depression, becoming healthy might mean incorporating a variety of things like counseling and treatment. Each one of us has to honestly evaluate where we are emotionally and physically and then make intentional decisions to live healthy lives.

Right now, becoming a healthier mom for my kids means that physically

I need to recommit to a consistent workout schedule. Once again, I have let deadlines and travel push aside the very thing I need to do to be a better mom for my kids. When my body is stronger because I have been working out regularly, I notice the extra burst of strength at the end of the day. Without my workouts, I'm dozing off by 9 p.m. And especially now, with so many teenagers in my house, I need that extra strength to engage their night-owl hearts.

To become healthier emotionally means several things for me right now. First, I realize that women my age are battling the emotional effects of oncoming menopause. Arrgggghhhh, I just can't stand thinking about it. If anyone could will it not to happen, I would will that for myself. I am too happy to become grumpy. I *love* being happy, and it kills me to think of hormones taking over my emotions and directing them to become sad. But I see it all around me, so that means I'm going to have to be alert. It could happen to me, and I'm just not willing to put my family through grumpy years. I've asked my husband to tell me honestly if I can't see it in myself. I want to address my emotional health proactively, doing whatever I need to do next to address what each new season brings.

> Your children need you to become healthy…We will have to be big girls who are able to say, "I'm not doing well and I want to get better."

Emotional health also means that I have to do the hard work of honest assessment. Am I short with people for no reason? Am I full of anxiety? Sad? Disconnected? Angry? I think emotional health has very strong ties to spiritual health, but for now, let's talk about an emotional unhealthiness that has taken hold because of wounds that need to be healed or emotional disorders that need professional treatment and care. It is not a sin to find yourself emotionally unhealthy. We can all get there for hundreds of different reasons. But it's wrong to know that you are emotionally unhealthy and refuse to seek help. For goodness' sake, your children need you to become healthy. None of us can bury our heads and hope it will just go away. We will have to be big girls who are able to say, "I'm not doing well and I want to get better." In the next chapter, we'll talk about becoming spiritually healthy, which is many times the first step to getting the emotional and physical help that you need.

As you already know, we're not going to get one more hour in our day.

We are going to wake up to the same children and the same tasks that need our attention. No one's schedule is going to change anytime soon. There are kids to raise and dinners to make and laundry to fold and their sweet lives that we don't want to miss. If I could buy more minutes I would, but we cannot manufacture any more minutes. The only thing you and I can do is to become stronger. With stronger bodies and minds to live each minute, we are getting and giving all that one woman can! And all that one woman can do is enough.

Reaching Their Hearts

I just don't want any of us to miss the sweetest days with our children because we have ignored our physical and emotional health. And I personally don't want to pass down the poor lifestyle that comes to the unhealthy. They will hold what I model for them in their hearts and be tempted to live it for themselves. *Mama was tired all the time. I guess that's just the way it's supposed to be. Mama was quick-tempered, so I can be too.* On and on. I fear that left alone, I will transfer an unhealthy body and unhealthy emotions to my sweet babies.

There are four reasons I desire to become an amazing woman. Those reasons stare at me across their cereal bowls every morning. My kids need a mom who is physically and emotionally healthy. Your kids do too.

26

Kids Need Their Mom...

To Become Spiritually Healthy

Unhealthy spirituality will sneak up on you. It's the kind of thing you might not see coming and then one day wake up to realize, *I am far away from God. And now that I think about it, I can't remember the last time I talked to Him. And my heart is empty. And I'm carrying so much pain. And life just feels so lonely and hard.*

You probably already know this, but when your spirit is unhealthy, you're not the only one who suffers. So does everyone around you, especially the children. An empty woman has nothing to give, and from her emptiness she can unintentionally give wounds instead of nurture.

In times when I was an empty mom, my words sounded more like shouting. My eyes cut a glare instead of giving tenderness. My actions were short and abrasive instead of loving. I was much more bossy than beautiful. I hate remembering the times I have been empty. Even more, I hate remembering the hurt on my children's faces when I have interacted with them from an empty spirit.

Maybe you've known some spiritually empty days too. And maybe some of you have been living like that for far too long. Your spirit aches for something different, but your routine hasn't responded to the need. If you and I could only do one thing to become better moms, this is the most powerful thing we could choose. To become a spiritually healthy woman is the sweetest gift we will ever give to our children.

Becoming healthy is going to require a few personal and intentional decisions. First, you and I will have to stop to assess where we are. How is it between you and God? What is your spiritual pulse today? Beating hard and fast, eager to grow in your relationship with Him? Or maybe you find your soul sluggish and slowing? Maybe the very first thing you will have to do is to ask God for a renewed spiritual desire. Without desire, not one of us will live in spiritual health.

Maybe discouragement has distanced you from God? Maybe a sin or a grievance? Maybe laziness? Today, assess your soul. If your desire has waned, pursue that first. Sometimes a time of prayer will renew me. Some days, just opening the Word of God will give me a fresh desire to know more of God. Other times, having coffee with a spiritually healthy woman will be just the boost my emptiness needs. Her passion is contagious. Her desire feeds mine.

> Wouldn't it be amazing to have God heal your wounded places right before your children's eyes?

Second, with a desire for greater spiritual health might come the realization that you have suffered spiritual wounds that need to be healed. To grow in health might require that you spend a season of time with a Christian counselor or meeting with a Christian support group. There is no shame in suffering wounds, but it is shameful to parent our children from our woundedness instead of searching for the healing that God can give. Wouldn't it be amazing to have God heal your wounded places right before your children's eyes? That will not happen until you choose healing. Jesus asked the invalid in John 5, "Do you want to be healed?" The question remains for us today. Will we continue in the pain, even indulging in self-pity, or do we want to be healed? To choose healing may require a journey, but oh my goodness, those children desperately need a healed mom.

Third, to become spiritually healthy, we will have to increase in Christlikeness. What that means is that spiritually healthy people are being changed by the Holy Spirit. But what happens all too often is that many people who follow Christ will not surrender themselves to the changing power of God. They get stubborn. And unwilling. And dig in their heels. And decide to stay just the way they are, thank you very much. But that is not what God desires for the woman who is growing up in her faith. You and I are called to become and to change. God wants each one of us to look more and more like His Son, less and less like the woman we have been.

To grow in Christlikeness means that we learn to respond when the Holy Spirit leads. Not next week or when I get around to it, but immediately.

God is so very gracious in how He shapes us. His love endures forever. His patience is without end. He longs for our souls to be fully devoted to Him. But the path to spiritual health is paved with obedience. Turning away from sinful behavior. Setting aside destructive habits. Choosing faith over despair. Accountability instead of independence. Living inside the family of God instead of trying to forge your way alone in this world.

And finally, you and I will have to choose spiritual health above all the other great endeavors that could easily distract us. It is such a wonderful thing to participate in the lives of others, to serve and to give, but something may have to go so that you can love your children from a spiritually healthy heart. I find myself in an incredibly busy time with teenagers at home and deadlines to meet. Right now, to choose spiritual health, which for me is the same as choosing sanity, means that I just can't serve outside my family and my work. I hope to have more opportunities to volunteer after they are grown, but right now spiritual health means not letting myself get distracted by the many wonderful things that come my way. I want to take meals to the hungry and gather books for the illiterate. I truly have a broken heart for impoverished people in countries around the world. I desperately want to help! But it's not my turn yet. My plate is full. To sacrifice spiritual health for the sake of more doing is not what God has called us to.

Reaching Their Hearts

For those of us with children, the most beautiful legacy we can build into their hearts is to become moms who parent them from spiritually healthy souls. May you and I decide to seek the Lord personally and respond to His leading quickly. I want my kids to live with the mom God had in mind when He gave them to me.

27

Kids Need Their Mom...

To Believe They Will Not Grunt Forever

Hey, sugar, how's your homework for tonight?" I cheerfully asked my 15-year-old son.

"Okay." With that, the one-word answers began.

"And how was your history test today?" the ever-inquisitive me kept going.

"Fine."

"And how about soccer practice—was it messy to practice in the rain this afternoon?"

Grunt.

"What did you say, honey?'

Half-grunt. My young man-child was completely out of words. He couldn't even fake it.

I went over to where he was sitting at the kitchen counter. Put my arms around him. Straightened his hair and kissed his head. "You're gonna come out of this fog one day," I lovingly said as I held onto him.

"Mom, I don't know what you're talking about. Why do you keep saying I'm in a fog?" he asked from his growing frustration.

"Well, baby, here's what I know. Most grown men with your IQ don't respond to every question with 'Huh. Yeah.' They use complete sentences, and then there is this amazing thing called conversation. We're going to have conversations again one day when you come out of the fog. Do you remember that your brother went into the fog about the same time as you? We should call 14 to 16 the foggy years. But your brother has come back to life, and that gives me hope. You are not going to grunt forever."

He kept sitting there like I was the craziest person breathing, but I continued, "Baby, here's what I have been learning about the mind of an adolescent. Neurologists say that during these years, your brain is rewiring. New connections are being formed. Your very countenance and personality are being shaped. So I've decided that while you're rewiring, you need the safest, most loving home ever. You need to know that grunting does not dissuade me. My unconditional love surrounds you. You're just walking through the brain fog, but we're all here with you. Your family kind of misses the old happy-go-lucky kid, but we're not going anywhere. We'll be with you the whole way."

Crazy, I did that whole scientific, brain rewiring, body-growing thing, and he didn't say a word. I think somewhere in his heart he knows he feels different. He can sense that things are changing inside of him. Some days he acts like the old chatty kid we used to have, and other days he's tired, distant, and barely able to grunt. Occasionally, it even feels like he's battling some anger and depression. Thankfully, this is my third teenager, and I am not jumping off of a bridge because he is grunting. And even though he lay in bed one night and promised me never to act like a weirdo, he has become his own little version of a weirdo. Still the cutest weirdo you've ever seen, but a weirdo nonetheless. It's his time. These are his years. I'm praying a lot, and thankfully, each day is another step out of the land of fog.

> We have the great privilege of believing that God is working out His plan for their lives in the dorky times and in the hard times and even the lost times.

My boys aren't the only ones struggling as they grow. It's hard to watch your little girl become the young woman who bursts into tears over a text message and then runs to her room to cry. Each one of my kids is facing the challenge of adjusting to their bodies, the new responsibilities they thought they always wanted, and this world that just won't go along with all their plans. In my house, I have a saying, "You can be a dork but sin not." I hold them close in these changing years, but I will not cover over sin or tolerate sinful choices. You can run to your room to cry, but you cannot scream at everyone in the house. You can live a couple of years in a foggy state, but you cannot choose sin just because your tiny mind is rewiring and reconnecting itself.

Growing up is tough. But it's just that, growing. Bless God, they aren't going to stall out in adolescence, grunting and crying for the rest of their lives. They're going to grow through it all. And honestly, I wouldn't want them acting like this anywhere else. So it's good they're here. Home. Safe. Loved. Sheltered.

As their mom, I think it's our job to keep believing in what they cannot yet see for themselves. We have the great privilege of believing that God is working out His plan for their lives in the dorky times and in the hard times and even the lost times. Our kids need their moms to have a vision that sees beyond today's poor attitude or yesterday's moodiness. They need to see us put our hope in God and not misplace our hope in their transitions, their mistakes, or even their accomplishments. We get to see up and over today's challenge. And then, with a heart full of hope and a lifetime full of experience, we get to keep pointing them in the direction of God.

Along the way, our children will need reminders of our commitment. *I love you even if you grunt. I will not run away when you make a mistake. I will stand beside you when everyone else is quiet. I will forgive you even when you have hurt me. I will pray for you. And believe in you. And wait for you. And above all these things, I will always love.*

Reaching Their Hearts

In this fickle world, our kids need a mom who is not wish-washy or easily dissuaded. A mom who still sees all that they can become. A mom who speaks gentle strength and assurance. Our children will transition in and out of different seasons of growth, but the most protective thing we can do is to let them do all their changing wrapped inside our love. They can cry and stomp and spit and walk away, but by golly, even when they are misguided and wrong, even when they are suffering the consequences they deserve, a mother's love remains.

So they grunt for a few years. A mom knows it won't last forever.

Kids Need Their Mom...

To Make a Big Deal Out of God

God has never been optional at my house. When I gave my heart and soul to become a follower of Jesus, I meant it. And for about 40 years, I have been learning how to mean it more every day. As the mom, I have the responsibility of setting the tone in our home, and as long as I am in charge, we are going to make a big deal out of God in this house. It's a joy and a privilege to follow Jesus Christ, and I want my kids to know that!

By big deal, I don't mean obnoxious or pushy or legalistic. I mean, God comes first. He is who we are living for. He is the one we serve. All our decisions are filtered through the biblical grid that comes from the Bible. I want our home and our lives to be lived for His glory, so God is a really big deal around here.

> God is everywhere here, and I love that for them.

In our home, I want my kids to grow up inside the presence of God. As parents, it's our place to invite the presence of God and to welcome the Lord into our homes by the very way we live our lives. Not perfectly, but surrendered. Not without sin, but truly forgiven. Not saints, but just a family who truly lives in awe of the Creator who wants a relationship with His created. What if our kids spent 18 or more years living in a house covered with prayer? Surrounded by faith and faith reminders? Sleeping sound underneath the shelter of grace? What would happen to the souls of kids who have been raised in a house where they make a big deal out of God? I'm praying that kind of childhood will shape my kids lives so that they can make an even bigger deal out of God than I do.

In our home, I want it to feel normal for them to be prayed for. To have spiritual conversations. To begin every meal with a grateful prayer to our Provider. We listen to all kinds of music in our house, but many days it's some kind of hip and cool praise music. I want them to know the words to that kind of music and sing in the shower and remember those songs when they are alone. It's good for them to push a Bible aside so they can eat their cereal and trip over stacks of theology books when they come into my office. God is everywhere here, and I love that for them.

For my kids, youth group and church activities have never been an option. We have tried to choose churches where the Bible is clearly taught and the student ministry is vibrant and alive. After we did, there were no options. We jumped in and brought the kids with us. In this house, church trumps most everything.

Soccer tournament or fall retreat? It's not a question around here, retreat. I tell the coach and take the blame, and not one thing inside of me ever regrets making the call. God is a bigger deal than soccer.

Ten-day middle school missions trip or driver's education? Yep, it's the missions trip without a blink. This year William's school is giving one opportunity to take driver's ed. It's during our church middle school missions trip. I have to think about it for only half a second to know that my boy needs ten days of serving the poor and thinking about other people way more than he needs a week of driver's ed with his friends. We'll sign up for driver's ed with strangers, but I will not sacrifice an opportunity for my kid to make a big deal out of God just for something that can be accomplished a hundred other ways. He'll get his driver's license, even if it's later, but my son needs to understand that some things, like serving God, matter more.

There are times we have to miss something, but I truly stand on my head to put God first, over all the other activities. This summer, Scott and I decided that even if we are out of town with the children, we need to get our family to church. This past beach vacation just happened to fall over Father's Day. We checked the schedules, ironed a few shirts, and rolled the whole family out of bed to go to church that Sunday morning. Our extended family filled a couple of pews at the small church where we vacation. The service was good, but what God did next surprised us beyond words.

The next morning, it "just happened" that the youth pastor from that small church brought some of his kids to the beach, in the exact spot where we had been all week. The pastor remembered our little tribe, introduced himself to everyone, and then invited our kids to Wednesday night Bible study. *Sweet,* I thought, *but these kids would never go to a strange youth group in a strange town.* Wednesday night rolled around, and amazingly, two of the boys persuaded all the kids to go. Scott and I dropped them off and drove around until time to pick them up. I was just waiting for the pitiful report. *No one talked to us. It was boring.* You know, the usual.

To our great surprise, our kids came running out of church with their cousins, smiles ear to ear, talking as fast as their mouths would go. *It was awesome! The message was powerful! The band was great! I'd love to go back! The youth pastor rocks!*

Scott and I learned a lesson that trip. We won't ever take another vacation from God. If we're out of town on a Sunday, we're tracking down a place where God is worshipped, the Bible is believed, and the family of God gets together. Since last summer, we've had some fun church adventures, especially the little mountain church where we sat in jeans and nice t-shirts among the suits and ties. Our family looked like an out-of-place rock band, but we blended in just fine when it came to praying and loving the Lord.

Reaching Their Hearts

Our kids need moms who will teach them that no matter what and no matter where, God is a really big deal.

29

Kids Need Their Mom...

To Keep Her Promise

N ope, we can't. Not right now. There is just no way we can have a dog. Unless we can pet-share with another family, we can't have a dog. We'd have to board that poor dog every weekend, and it wouldn't be right." Oh, the years of painful conversations I've had with my children, who desperately and understandably wanted a dog. But I was a single mom who was sure I could not handle one more thing. And when I'd feel weak and almost give in, my neighbors would talk me back to sanity. "You cannot have a dog," they'd firmly declare. And so, for about eight years, I promised, "One day."

When Scott came into our lives, he too promised the children that we'd have a dog after we were married and settled. There was a wedding, a move, a new church and new school, and finally, time to keep the promise. Scott and I searched online for just the right kind of family dog for us. Not too big. Not too little. Nonshedding would be a plus. Really cute was a must. Scott wanted a girl, and that was fine with me.

We eventually found a lady in Virginia who had a beautiful litter of Cavanese puppies, and there were two females in the bunch. I was shocked to find out that we had to first be approved before we could see pictures of the puppies. Thankfully, we were approved. The owner emailed the pictures of the girls to us. Scott was at his work looking at them, I was here in the house. And wouldn't you know it, they were both so cute and we have so many kids, Scott said, "I'm fine if we get both of them." So two girls it was!

But how to tell the children, who had been waiting for eight years? Well, it seemed like a surprise was in order. A little surprise wouldn't do. This one would have to be big. The puppies were about six hours away and wouldn't be ready to come home with us until the weekend before Thanksgiving. We decided to take the kids on a fun family get-away road trip. We loaded the kids into the car with overnight bags and stopped on the way to get Taylor at college. "Where are we going?" they asked.

"Oh, just some family time. I was thinking we could do a little historical sightseeing here in Virginia," I told them.

They all smiled at Scott and me politely. We've never taken a historical sightseeing trip, so I'm sure they all thought we had lost our minds. That night we drove for hours to get to the George Washington Inn. Historical. Tucked them in and then the next morning they swam in the historical George Washington pool and walked down historical streets to colonial houses and even to one of George Washington's offices. We took pictures, ate lunch, and just played up the history.

> Before I say, "I promise," I have to be sure that I mean it. That it's possible. That I am able.

The time came to head toward the horse farm where the dog breeder lived. As we were making our way through the tiny, winding roads, William piped up from the backseat with a forced kind of gratefulness, "Mom, thanks for taking us on this historical trip."

"You're welcome, honey. It's fun, huh?"

"Where are we going now?" Taylor asked.

"A historical horse farm. Won't that be fun!" I responded.

Taylor said all she could think was *Mom knows I don't like riding horses. I can't believe we are going to ride horses. Ugh. I guess I'd just better be nice and go along with it.*

We turned onto the beautiful drive to the farm, and sure enough, there were horses behind fences along both sides of the road. I looked in the back, and the kids were changing their shoes for horse riding. Scott and I tried to hold ourselves together with everything we had. They had no idea what we were doing.

We pulled up where the owner had instructed, and she came out to greet us. The kids got out of the car and meandered over to the building, halfhearted about all the horse riding we were getting ready to do. The breeder said hi to all of them, and then she said, "Come inside while I get your puppies."

Well, four children almost fainted.

Us? Puppies for us? We're not riding horses? We're getting puppies? We can keep them? We're taking them home?

And then she came through the door with the two cutest ten-week-old sisters you have ever seen. Tears. Joy. One of the all-time happiest moments our family has ever known. It was such a sweet day. The children were beside themselves. Scott and I were beaming and wiping tears and hugging the puppies and the kids. Promise kept. Finally, promise kept.

It matters that we keep our promises to our children, even if it takes eight years. If I say to one of my children, "I promise you that I will do this," they know they can count on me. I may have to delay the keeping of my promise, but I always keep my word. What that means for me is that I do not make promises lightly. Before I say, "I promise," I have to be sure that I mean it. That it's possible. That I am able.

Reaching Their Hearts

In this world of broken trust and good intentions, our children need their moms to be promise keepers. How will they learn unless we show them? How will they become truth tellers unless we have taught them? The lesson goes deep inside of them to that place that builds security and trust. Mom means what she says. Mom keeps her promises. Mom thinks enough of me to keep her word.

And I pray the lesson is contagious. May all our kids learn how to keep their promises. This world will be a different place if each one passes the integrity of promise keeping to the next generation.

30

Kids Need Their Mom...

To Wait on Them Hand and Foot...When They Are Sick

There are people in this world who want to be left alone when they are sick. I know because I am married to one of them. But I had not encountered these people before, so I thought everyone ought to be pampered and fussed over when they felt bad. At least that's what my mama taught me.

I was raised by a mom who is a nurse, so my brothers and I couldn't get away with anything growing up. No fake fevers. No mercy for a little sniffle. There was no "kinda feeling bad" at our house. You were either sick enough to miss school and every other activity for that day, or you weren't. But when we had been diagnosed truly sick, my mom and all her tender nursing skills were the sweetest gifts.

There is no capacity for nursing inside of me, much to my mom's disappointment, but I had such a great role model that when my kids are sick, I pretend I'm her and pull out all her gentle nursing tricks.

First, there is the sofa conversion. My kids have never wanted to be shut away in their rooms, so I usually convert the sofa in the family room into their sickbed. I make the sofa up with comfy sheets, warm blankets, and fluffed pillows. The TV remote is close, but most importantly, I am close. I think they just like to hear me stirring around in the kitchen, checking in on them often. Tucking and retucking. Stroking their hair. Taking their temperature. Washing their face with a warm washcloth. Keeping their toes warm with socks and a heating pad.

Maybe because my mom made such a fuss over us when we were sick,

I remember how loved her attention made me feel. There is just something about knowing your mom is trying to make you comfortable that gives a comfort all its own. If there is any way, I cancel my day when one of the children is at home sick. We slow the pace to focus on rest and healing. I'll build a fire for coziness. Light the candles. Dim the lights. Sick days are the time I let them have anything that might stay down or feel good. Popsicles all day. Ice cream for breakfast. Ginger ale. Homemade chicken soup. Whatever it takes to nourish the weak.

> We can teach our children how to care for others who suffer when we sincerely and lovingly care for them.

A few days ago, my 20-year-old called from Arizona to tell me she was sick. She missed her mom, and I wished I could get to her just to give her sweet mama comfort. Instead of making homemade soup, the best I could do was write her the email below:

Sweet Tay, I am so sorry you are sick today. It's awful to know your baby feels bad and you can't get to them. In case you may have forgotten what to do when you're sick, here is your mama checklist to follow:

1. Sleep as much as you can. Sleeping helps, really.

2. Test your ability to eat by nibbling a cracker. Go slow. Not too much or you could pay later. Yuck.

3. Sugary drinks go down better than water. Sprite and stuff like that.

4. Eat popsicles for breakfast. Unexplainable, but it makes things better.

5. Call your ma every so often and tell her you feel bad. It just helps to tell your mom.

6. Take the medicine that might help you feel better. You don't have to be tough and suffer through the symptoms.

7. Take a bath on day two of being sick. Really, do not skip this step.

8. If you are the same or worse on Day 3, it's time to head to the doctor or walk-in clinic. Something is not going away!

9. Did I mention sleep? Keep doing that.

10. Lay your head on your pillow and remember that you are loved by a really big family. And they miss your sick face.

From the one who has rocked you through every icky thing and now has to trust God to rock you in His arms instead. I'm sure He'll do a good job—it's just that I wish I were there to help Him!

I love you, honey.

I am not usually a proponent of spoiling our children, but in their sickness, I think it's time to pull out all the stops. Spoil them rotten, I say. It's time to wait on them hand and foot and to teach them about service and unconditional love. When people cannot help themselves, it is a blessing to them and to God to show genuine concern and attention. We can teach our children how to care for others who suffer when we sincerely and lovingly care for them on their worst days.

Reaching Their Hearts

Sick days are beautiful days for giving unconditional love. I may not kiss my child on their germy face, but I will kiss their head and massage their aches and never remove my touch. Everybody in this world needs somebody who will move closer when they are hurting. A sick day at home with my precious child has always turned into a gift to me. They let me hold them longer and rock for hours and snuggle closer. They need me, and I have the great privilege of responding to their need with tenderness and compassion.

We never want any of our children to suffer with sickness, but on those days when it's inevitable, I think kids need their moms to show them lavish compassion and grace.

31

Kids Need Their Mom...

To Tell Them to Buy Another Token and Keep Swinging

Last year, William decided to try out for the baseball team at his school.
It had been at least four years since he and Grayson had played baseball for our neighbor's team back in Tennessee. So the week before tryouts, we found our gloves and started to throw the ball around. The day before tryouts, after a soccer game, he persuaded me to take him to our town's batting center. After we got there, we realized the place was packed with real baseball people. Big players, little players, coaches of all kinds, and lots of moms and very serious baseball dads. His friend Marco met us there. Marco has been playing baseball for many years. Marco's dad came too.

William and I had no idea we were going to such an intense baseball center. I had Googled the place and thought we were headed to some batting cages beside the putt-putt, like back in Tennessee. But no, this place was a big deal. I said to William, "What do you think?" imagining that he might be intimidated by all the kids who had been playing baseball the way he had been playing soccer. Unfazed by all the hoopla, William said, "It's cool."

We bought tokens. William borrowed Marco's bat and went into the first cage. A machine pitched 20 balls to him. Twenty times he swung the bat. Twenty times he missed. Ugh. I was dying for him. But here's the thing, William never acted like it got to him. He came out of the cage and wanted to try again. Marco went next, and he met 20 pitches with 20 hits. Very impressive. Then William took his second turn. Marco's dad gave him some pointers, and he went back for 20 more swings at the air. My mama heart was hurting for him. After he was done, I asked, "What do you think?" expecting he'd say, "I don't have it." But William almost yelled to me, "I LOVE it!" *Huh, you love it?* I thought to myself. *You missed 40 pitches in a row.* But this mom just kept standing there smiling.

Then there was the third token, and he barely whacked one ball into the ground, missing the other 19. I think he was bummed when we left that night, but for some reason, his spirit never seemed broken.

> My boy taught me a new mom lesson. Keep swinging... until your passion finds its sweet spot.

The next day, the first day of tryouts was rained out, so after school, he begged me to take him back to the batting center. We decided to start with a slower pitching machine. And unbelievable, he hit 20 for 20. Next token, another 20. Faster machine, 20 more. Even faster machine, 20 more. That second day, he swung the bat 120 times and hit all 120 balls. Crazy, amazing. Where was the kid who whiffed the day before? He was gone. Derek Jeter had shone up the next day.

William taught me such a powerful lesson those two days. I never told him to give up, and obviously I drove him back to the batting cages, but I honestly didn't have any hope for the kid. Driving home that second day I said to him, "Can I tell you how proud I am of you! I don't care if you make the baseball team this year or ever. I'm just *so proud* that the day after you missed 59 balls, you wanted to go back and prove something to yourself. You wanted to keep trying. What a great lesson for me. I would have probably given up after 8 misses. I would have whined about the bat or the blisters or the intense people, but you just wanted to keep swinging until you connected."

That day in the baseball cages, my boy taught me a new mom lesson. Keep swinging. If you think it's in your heart, and your mind tells you that you can, keep swinging until your passion finds its sweet spot. I wish I'd been more vocal that day. I wish I had given William encouraging words and cheered him to keep going back, but I didn't. I didn't think he had the skill. What I found out is that he had heart. It was his determination that taught me how to mother him next time. Next time, I'll yell to that kid, "Try again, honey! Keep swinging at the thing your heart desires."

Maybe I'm supposed to care more, but I couldn't care less about baseball tryouts or making a team. I love sports for the children, and I want them to have fun, but I don't really give a hoot about what level they play or how intense their game is. I think the pressure to perform in sports is borderline ridiculous. Maybe I feel that way because I have never been able to connect the bat with the ball or shoot a free throw worth anything. William made the team that year and played a little, sat on the bench a little, and learned a lot about supporting players who are better than you. But nothing that season compared with the batting cage lesson. Winning in sports is fun, but our kids will win at life because their attitude is right and they don't quit on the first 20 tries.

Reaching Their Hearts

And so, maybe in this life we can teach our children there are times when we will miss 59 times in a row. And our hearts will sink. And our bodies will be weary. But when you really want to do something, I have learned from William, buy another token and keep swinging.

Kids Need Their Mom...

To Pray Them Home
and for the Will of God

When our son Grayson was 14, he decided to go and live with his dad. It is such an understatement to tell you that I was devastated for a million reasons. Now, three years later, I can look back with the corrected vision of hindsight and see God's hand. Even though we are still learning so much about the journey we have traveled, we now believe those hard years were meant for good, both for Grayson and for his dad. I couldn't have said that three years ago. At the beginning, it was like my world blew up. I desperately tried to grab onto my son, but he was gone.

After we moved Grayson into his dad's house and our family moved to North Carolina without him, all I knew was to pray. So every time I prayed, I ended my prayer, "Lord, bring Grayson home." Sometimes I would add, "Your will be done," but truthfully, I just wanted my boy, God's will or not. As the months went by, I figured everyone was tired of hearing me beg God to bring Grayson home, so I stopped saying it out loud and just kept quietly praying, "God, please bring Grayson home." I am not the only one who prayed. Grandparents prayed. My husband prayed. My brothers prayed. And even though I prayed, I couldn't honestly see any movement from God. I stopped bringing it up to Grayson when

> I finally had the strength to say to him, "Baby, I am learning the hardest lesson of my life. I am learning how to trust God to care for my son."

we talked. He always said he wanted to stay where he was. But in my heart, I kept praying.

I do have to confess that while I was stubbornly praying for the only answer I could imagine, God began a painful and deep refining work in me. He was teaching me to trust Him with my son, even if I disagreed with every part of the plan and the painfully long process. For months I screamed and begged. Cried and prayed. Paced and pouted. And then one day, I knew God wanted me to stand up on something higher than my pity party and look at my son through His eyes. He wanted me to act big instead of small. He wanted me to have vision instead of blindness.

At my next visit with Grayson, I finally had the strength to say to him, "Baby, I am learning the hardest lesson of my life. I am learning how to trust God to care for my son. I now realize that I want you to stay with your dad as long as God directs you to do that. I want you to learn everything you are supposed to be learning. I want your good more than I want my own satisfaction and comfort. Grayson, please know that even though I wish everything was different, you have my blessing. Son, I love you." I remember dropping him off back at his dad's and believing he was gone forever. Oh, how deep was that grief.

Months went by, and my prayers became less selfish. *When it's Your time, God. If it's Your will, God. Whatever is best for my son, God. Oh, make me stronger. Give me wisdom. Help me see all of this like You do.* But you know I am just a mom, and each one of those more mature prayers always ended with the desire of my heart, *Lord, bring my beautiful boy home.*

Almost a year ago, God brought Grayson home, but He did not bring home the same old Grayson. He delivered to us a brand new Grayson. One that I could not have imagined I'd ever meet. Grayson came to North Carolina completely changed by the power and presence of God. He has a passionate relationship with Jesus. He is sold out. 180. A different kid who is becoming an amazing man. In those two years with his dad, God worked a miracle in Grayson's heart. That kid is radically and completely changed. And somewhere in all of that change, when it was time, Grayson said God told him to come home.

The next year when my oldest daughter, Taylor, moved to Arizona, my broken heart knew what to do. Trust God with His babygirl. Pray without ceasing. Pray for God's will sooner and entrust my comfort to the Holy

Spirit, not the circumstances. This past fall I thought Taylor would stay in Arizona forever, and one month later she was home.

I don't think any of my kids have acted like prodigals, but they have been away from me in ways that I could not control or oversee or guide. I am sure that come-home-and-God's-will prayers are exactly the kind of prayers God teaches the moms of prodigals too.

My friend Carlye had a prodigal boy named Rob. For 18 years, Carlye and the whole family prayed for Rob to return to his senses and come home. They all learned more than they ever wanted to know about trusting God with circumstances and children beyond their control. Eventually their prayers were answered when Rob went home to be with the Lord early one Valentine's Day morning. Even in her grief, Carlye finally had the assurance her son was okay. He was home with the Lord. Healed. Loved. Redeemed. He had gone home and all in God's will.

Reaching Their Hearts

Praying God's will for our children will surely mean something different for each family, but I believe a mom is supposed to pray. Pray them out of compromising circumstances. Pray them into havens of grace. Pray for protection and purpose and calling, and all our prayers are to be covered by the powerful surrender to God's will.

Grayson's leaving taught me to pray in ways I never wanted to know. But God's answers have taught me to trust Him with my children. I have seen with my own eyes the amazing power of God to transform lives, both Grayson's and mine.

The afternoon Grayson came home I waited in the kitchen with tears streaming down my face, fresh sheets on his bed, and a peach cake sitting on the counter. I promised God that His faithfulness to us would not go unseen. I would shout to the world, GLORY TO GOD, who hears the stubborn prayers of moms and teaches them lessons about His will being done on this earth.

Oh, mamas, let us pray our children home. May His will be done.

Kids Need Their Mom...

To Be a "Groovy" Mom

AnnaGrace must have been in the first grade. Our little group arrived at school in the usual morning carpool kind of way. Kids fresh and ready. Me with a mug of coffee, ponytail, and gym shorts. I was coming back to the school in a few hours for a party in AnnaGrace's class. As she kissed me goodbye, I told her, "I'll see you in just a bit."

"Mom," she said, "when you come back to school today, can you be a groovy mom?"

"Yes, honey, I'll be a groovy mom," I said, smiling to myself about my babygirl's instruction.

Groovy mom. I cannot be that most of the time. Like today for instance, I am sitting in a coffee shop writing to you, and I am clean. I have a clean face and clean hair that happens to still be wet, and I am wearing clean clothes. But I am not groovy today. I am comfortable, and I'm wearing no makeup in hopes that some of the expensive medicine I have put on my face will have a chance to work today. Honestly, I almost look awful, but I am hiding in my writing cave and working, so what does it matter?

> Groovy means that I try to look nice at their events. That I don't go "granny" on them.

Home is the place where every member of my family can relax and be themselves. We don't dress up at home. Very little makeup is worn at home. No one is judged for bed head or mismatched clothes or for a few days of sweatpants. Home is easy and comfortable and cozy. But what I have come to realize it that my kids really need me to pull it together sometimes. They like it when I try to look nice. They're proud of me when I fit in my workouts or tell them I spent an hour exercising. They want me to be a groovy mom, not all the time, but sometimes.

It's easy to understand why a lot of moms give up. For goodness' sake, I get it! We are tired and our bodies are changing and our family's schedules can become downright overwhelming. I see the moms at school and church. They are all just as worn out as I am. And being groovy is just about the last thing on their minds. Surviving is big. Being nice to people is high on the list. But groovy…most of us don't have time to think about it.

So what's a busy mom to do? I think we ought to give them groovy sometimes. Groovy means that I try to look nice at their events. That I don't go "granny" on them and always show up in granny shoes and ten-year-old clothes. Now I do have several pairs of granny shoes, and lots of clothes older than ten years. As a matter of fact, I'm wearing a pair of those shoes and one of those shirts right now. But when I'm going for groovy, that means I need to try to do better. Groovy means updating myself for my kids, even if I couldn't care less. And honestly, most days now, in the middle of life, with all the beautiful freedom I feel to be real, I don't really care about groovy.

After I finish here in the coffee shop, I'm going to run by the house, change my shoes and throw on a little makeup because AnnaGrace and I have some shopping to do. I know she'll never say a word if I show up looking like this, but I do know she likes for me to try. Not to mention, I'm sure my husband likes the occasional groovy version of me too. I'm going home to change to communicate to her that I care about my appearance when I'm with her. To make her proud that I'm her mom. And to model for her the care of her appearance. I hope you are hearing me. This is not a rule or a have-to. It's a gift we give to our children.

Sometimes women give up caring about their appearance and style because they've gotten discouraged about their circumstances or fallen into a pattern of laziness. How easy is that? Who wants to buy the new current fashion in the size you don't want to wear? Not me! But maybe we buy a few inexpensive things until we're back in the old cute clothes in the closet. Sweatpants and sports clothes are just not groovy. We've got to try, at least a little. I want to encourage us all, if not for ourselves, for our children, can we try! Please don't read this and translate it to say, "Spend more money on yourself." That's fine and dandy if you want to, but that's not the intent of being groovy. The heart of this idea is about caring how you present yourself to your children, especially at their public events.

That day when AnnaGrace asked me to come back to school groovy, she wasn't saying, *I don't love you the way you are.* She was saying, *I will love you no matter what, but I love showing off my cool mom.* She wanted me to go home and put on my hip jeans, cute boots, and some kind of fun top. She wanted me to do my makeup, style my hair, and smell like her favorite perfume. That day at school, I walked in and she ran to hold onto me. "Mom," she whispered, "you look awesome." My kids are all a little older now, but I know it still means a lot to them.

Reaching Their Hearts

So what do you say? The next time you need to buy something to wear, go for groovy. The kids might faint, but they'll love knowing that their mom cares and she tries.

Kids Need Their Mom...

To Teach Them How to Know the Voice of God

We live in a loud house. I have four fairly loud talkers. Music is usually going in several rooms at one time. The dogs bark. The television roars. The Xbox pings. The doorbell rings. A lot of input is going into the hearts and minds of my children. Not to mention the texts and tweets and posts. The kids at school. Their teachers. Lots and lots of sounds and voices and streams of information to fill their little heads.

But if I could give my children one thing that will filter every distracting sound, I would give them the gift of discernment. I want them to know the voice of God. I want them to learn what God sounds like so that they can follow Him with a firm and unwavering commitment. They also need to know the difference between the voice of God and the voice of the Accuser, who is the deceiver.

> I am trying to build a strong biblical grid into the minds of my kids.

As they are growing, I am trying to build a strong biblical grid into the minds of my kids. With that grid in place, I pray they will able to sift through the input of this world and then discern what sounds like the voice of God and what does not. I want them to read the newpaper headlines or watch an interview on television and using their grid, be able to make wise decisions, form biblical opinions, and choose right causes with which to serve.

What happens to many of us is that we have not learned the difference between the voice of our Father, God, and the voice of Satan, our accuser. Even children who have been raised by Christian parents many times cannot tell you the difference between the voice of God and the voice of the Accuser. So for some of us, we will have to learn ourselves so that we can give this powerful lesson to our children.

Here are just some of the differences between the voice of God, who speaks to us through the Holy Spirit, and the voice of the Accuser:

> The Holy Spirit will bring conviction.
> The Accuser wants to bring shame.
>
> The Holy Spirit speaks to us about freedom and
>   release from our sin.
> The Accuser wants to keep us in bondage.
>
> The Holy Spirit convicts us clearly and specifically about
>   an action, attitude, or misguided belief.
> The Accuser promotes confusion and blame.
>
> The Holy Spirit prompts us toward confession and
>   repentance so we can hear God's heart of love.
> The Accuser wants us to believe that we are eternally
>   condemned.
>
> God might say, "You didn't tell the truth."
> The Accuser would say, "You are a liar."
>
> The Holy Spirit wants to clear away all that distracts you
>   from living a beautiful life with God.
> The Accuser wants to keep you distracted...for the rest
>   of your life.*

Discernment means that we have come to understand the character of God and His heart toward us, His beloved.

If my child comes home and says, "I'm a loser," I have the perfect opportunity to teach this lesson about discernment. Maybe I would respond to them like this:

> Baby, that's what Satan wants you to believe about yourself. He
> is the one whispering that lie into your head. But I want you to

---

* Angela Thomas, *Do You Think I'm Beautiful?* (Nashville, TN: Lifeway Press, 2007), p. 60.

understand something. What you just said to me is not what God thinks of you. I want you to learn how to hear God's voice instead of that lie. God calls you beautiful. He says you are His beloved. You are wonderfully made. You are not a loser because the Bible says you can do all things through Christ who give you strength.

Maybe you are just beginning to learn the difference between the voice of God and the voice of the Accuser. Lean into that lesson. Pursue time with others who can guide you. Attend a Bible study that focuses on hearing God's voice. (I highly recommend Priscilla Shirer's study *Discerning the Voice of God.*)

Become a mom who is learning to listen to God.

Reaching Their Hearts

The gift of discernment is a character trait that will direct the future decisions our children will make. Learning to discern God's voice will be life-transforming for them. May we become moms who know the difference between God, who is love, and Satan, who is lies. And then, let us teach our children well.

Kids Need Their Mom...

To Believe in Their Strengths and Speak Life into Their Gifts

The other day I had such a sweet conversation with my 20-year-old daughter, Taylor. As we've done many times before, we were talking about her future, what she wants to do, and what she likes. I told her, "Honey, you have strong influencer gifts. You are quick to discern and quick to make a good decision. God gave you a heart of compassion, especially for the poor and abused." I kept going on about her personality traits, and after a few minutes, Taylor asked, "Mom, what do you see in the other kids?" I told her about some of the strengths her brothers and sister have, things that are different from hers but still so very great. I don't think she had realized that all this time I had been trying to learn about each one of them.

To be a student of our children means that we learn as much as we can about their individual personalities, their gifting, and the way they process. As I examine each one of my children, it is so fun for me to learn about God's unique wiring inside of them. A couple of them have the same eyes, and the other two have the same hair, but for the most part, I have four uniquely created people. Each one bearing different strengths. Each one looking out at the world with their own perspective, longings, and ambition. Our kids need a mom who will believe in their strengths and speak life into their gifts. We are privileged to be their observer. Their encourager. Their biggest fan.

My first years as a single mom was a time of great brokenness for me. There were so many emotions—shame, embarrassment, and just plain discouragement. While I tried not to show it to my children, on the inside I had given up. I'll never forget how it felt as a grown woman to have some wise men say to me, "Angela, here are the gifts we see inside of you. We believe in you. We think God is going to use even your brokenness to glorify Him with your life." The words of those men were healing words to me. But even more, they inspired me. In much the same way, we have the great privilege of inspiring and challenging our own children to use what they have been given to live for God's glory.

Here's where we may have to caution ourselves. Sometimes as parents, we can get caught up in the mistaken idea that our children can grow up to do anything if only they will work hard enough and believe in themselves. Not true. Our children have been wired with different strengths and abilities. Everyone can't become anything. If my parents had mistakenly believed I could become a great singer and challenged me to keep training and trying, we would have all beaten our heads against the wall. I cannot sing. Nada. Maybe with training, I could have become tolerable, but the gift was not given to me. God did not put a singing voice in my design package. Neither did I get quick hand/eye coordination. A sweet jump shot. Or the inclination toward craftiness. Not only is it futile to encourage our children concerning gifts they have not been given, it's downright wrong.

> Kids need us to survey the lay of the land and help them navigate their choices based on their strengths.

Our job is to look for their strengths and champion the very best of who they can become. This world of unfair comparison is discouraging for everybody, kids and grownups alike. Our kids need a mom who never gives up on them. A mom who can see past a bad grade and reroute a dead-end choice. They need us to survey the lay of the land and help them navigate their choices based on their strengths.

When Taylor went off to college, I knew what she needed was a first-semester victory, not a challenge. She needed to lead with her strengths that year. I told her not to take anything hard. "Take the things that come easy for you, like speech. Get adjusted to college life and living in a dorm." She needed to use that time to build her confidence, not become overwhelmed and discouraged. I have other children who might be ready for the challenge of their academic lives when they go off to college, but prayerfully, we'll be able to see their strengths and be wise about their weaknesses.

As moms, we get to be home base. I know you remember the game of baseball. The batter practices all season. He overcomes the stress and exerts his skill to get a hit at bat. He runs and maneuvers to get around all the bases. And the reward is finally touching home base. The fans go wild. The coach is beaming. The team is cheering. He made it home. There is just something about touching home that makes it all worth it.

I want to be the place where my kids touch home. No matter what they choose to do in their lives, whether my kids come across the plate limping, or sliding, or victory-dancing, I want to be the one cheering wildly with uncompromising belief in who they are and what they can be. When I was growing up, a call with my dad would be like touching home. He believed in me, still does. I have a friend in my life, and every interaction with her is like touching home. She speaks life into my weariness and reminds me of the strengths God placed inside of me. I want to be that for each one of my children.

When they are older, I pray my kids will zoom around the challenges of their lives and keep remembering to touch home base. I pray that as long as I live, God will use me to refresh their spirits, speak life into their callings, and remind them I have never stopped believing in all God has made them to be. No matter where and no matter what, I will always be cheering wildly from the stands. Hootin' and hollerin' over all they are and all they are yet to be.

Reaching Their Hearts

Everybody needs somebody to believe in them. I am blessed to be the chief believer of four.

36

Kids Need Their Mom...

To Make a Home
Where Grace Lives

Y ou can grow grass after the kids are raised," my daddy said.

I was a single mom who had just managed to purchase a house that was perfect for me and the children. Not only did it fit our needs and happen to be in the neighborhood where their friends lived, it had been well taken care of. Really. The house was older, but it was immaculate. Nothing to fix. No peeling paint or stains on the carpet. It was exactly what a woman who is not handy needed. There wasn't even one weed or bare spot in the yard, mainly because the former owners were amazing yard people. I was thrilled to buy the house but intimidated by the challenge to keep up their standards.

The day we moved in, my dad and I were standing on the back deck, tired from moving all the boxes but so very happy about the new home for me and the kids. As we stood there soaking up the summer evening, the boys came racing around the house on their bicycles with all their neighborhood friends behind them. It was like we moved in and someone yelled, "Gentlemen, start your engines."

My first thought was one of sheer panic, *the grass!* I guess my dad read my mind as he watched the boys go around the house the second time. He looked over at me and spoke the sweet truth of grace. "You can grow grass after the kids are raised." He was right. So very right. My natural inclination was stress. About the grass, for goodness' sake. But his truth cut through my stress like a knife. My boys were the happiest I could remember seeing them. So what if they built a dirt track around our new home. I'd have the rest of my life to grow grass.

My daddy just might be one of the smartest men in the whole, entire world. That day on my deck about ten years ago helped shape the parenting style I believe God desires. I have decided that our home should be the place where grace lives. This firstborn, organized, neat and tidy mom has learned that a home filled with grace is the home that honors God and His gift of our family.

More grace means that everybody's welcome, even when they track in mud and pile their snowy clothes by the back door. Grace means that grades are important, having a job is a blessing, keeping the yard pretty is a goal, but love covers everything. Some days grace means setting aside all the things that need to be done for the great joy of loving my family and friends. I treasure the saying, "There is an art to leaving some things undone, so that the greater thing can be done."

> A house of grace means you can make a mistake here, and we will not keep holding it against you.

In our house of grace, I'm always going for laughter, but sarcasm is not allowed. Honestly, I hate sarcastic comments and attitudes. I can't stand to be with people who pick on each other and belittle each other. I hear them say it's all in fun, but it has never made sense to me. Life is too hard, and our home is not going to be the place where it's hard to be. Being at home should be easy, not stressful or quarrelsome. No one gets picked on in my house. I can't stand it.

We're going to look for God in our circumstances so that we can put our hope in His faithfulness instead of getting stuck in our disappointments. We aren't going to look for someone to blame but learn to take a humble responsibility for our own shortcomings. I want my family to read the daily newspaper with discernment, not allowing its contents to sour their souls or give false hope toward the attractions of this world. I pray that the grace in our home will settle their souls and fix their minds on the only One who can guide, restore, and renew. That where there is grace, there will also be peace.

A house of grace means you can make a mistake here, and we will not keep holding it against you. You are free to grow and mature. Becoming a new and better person is encouraged and applauded. Liking new things is allowed. Changing your mind is okay.

In a grace-filled house, you can come to breakfast with a bed head, and no one will snicker. You can wear your worn-out pajamas and your icky old hat, and we're all going to love you just the same. There are no perfect people in our house, not even close. But each one is loved in this house of grace, just as they are, right where they are. I pray it's the kind of love God had in mind when He created this beautiful connection called family.

I think that in a house full of grace, you should be free to dance a little more and sing a little louder. I hope people drive by our house and wonder what in the world is always going on here. Cars in the driveway. People going in and out. Lights staying on a little later. We sit on the front steps and talk. And wave good-bye. And kiss a lot.

When my kids run in the back door this afternoon, drop their backpacks at the kitchen table, and head to the pantry for a snack, oh, how I want those people I love to be drenched in the good grace of God. What I know about grace is that you cannot impart what you do not possess. A house of grace will begin with you and me.

Reaching Their Hearts

May we receive for ourselves the very grace God has called us to in His Son, Christ Jesus. A grace that forgives our sin. A grace that lets us begin again and again. A grace that keeps believing in all we can be. A grace that sees the woman God has always known you could be.

So quick! Let us become women of grace so that we are able to make a home where grace lives.

37

Kids Need Their Mom...

To Throw Down the "MOM Card"

The "MOM card" is the final say. Done. Over. Decision made.

As often as I have been able, I have tried to let my children make their own decisions. When they were younger, I would give them a couple of options and then let them choose. Macaroni and cheese or spaghetti? Play Doh or Legos? Ponytail or pigtails? There wasn't very much reason to throw down the MOM card except for their own protection. Like the time I stopped six boys from skateboarding off of the two-story jungle gym in the backyard. The second I looked out the kitchen window and saw those boys lined up for the rooftop slalom trick of their lives, I ran out the back door and threw down the MOM card for all six of them. No way. Everybody down. I don't have time to go to the hospital today.

The MOM card is the trump card in my mothering deck of tricks. Honestly, I don't use it very often, but what I have heard from my kids is that they are grateful for the times I have stepped in and made a firm decision on their behalf, even if it didn't seem to go their way at first.

Because I want to have a relationship with my children, I want to talk to them, hear their opinions, and listen to their ideas, I don't use the MOM card very often. But there are times when I have to be the mom and make the call.

I'll throw down the MOM card every time I feel I need to protect my children. It's the old, "I don't care what everyone else is doing, here's how we're going to do it in our family." For years, I threw down the MOM card about video games, the Internet, and social media. I said no and that was the final word. I don't like violence, so that ruled out a lot of games, and my kids weren't old enough to navigate the Internet or social media with wisdom.

Today, I've let the rope out on a lot of those things, mostly because the children have shown great integrity in their choices. My youngest daughter, who is 13, has actually decided not to pursue social media even though most of her friends are online. At least for the time being, she has heard me talk about this enough to decide she just doesn't want the distraction. I secretly think she likes being the youngest and wants to stay that way for as long as possible. My 15-year-old tech-savvy son has a Facebook account, but he is not allowed to have a wall where others can post to his page. I just don't think he's ready for that, and I've done enough surfing to know some of the things kids his age are posting. No thanks. The children are not allowed to use the computer privately, and for years the only computer in the house was my traveling laptop that went everywhere with me. It was only last summer that I bought a computer to put in the kitchen because the schools require kids to have access for most of their at-home assignments. It was hard for them to finish their papers when I was out of town with the only computer.

> This is the haven where I invite the Spirit of God to abide. I'll use the MOM card all day long to keep our house clean and honorable to the Lord.

I'll use the MOM card to resolve differences or deal with indecision. AnnaGrace and some friends were signed up for an important retreat weekend with the youth group at church. Three days before the retreat, a girlfriend at school announced she was having a birthday sleepover. The girls were torn about what to do. They wanted to go on the retreat, and they didn't want to miss the fun birthday party. AnnaGrace hemmed and hawed about what to choose. I understood her indecision. She wanted to do both. Finally, one afternoon she looked at me and said, "Mom, will you use the MOM card?" I was glad to step in and put her out of her misery. "You should keep your first commitment," I said. MOM card on the table. Decision was made. Daughter relieved. I'm sure she said to her friends, "Mom said…" which is exactly what I've told her to do. Blame me.

Other times, I'll use the MOM card when an explanation to the children is inappropriate. I haven't let my boys go to sleep-away sports camps. We always choose the day camp option instead. I realize that bad things don't happen everywhere, but I've just heard too many things about hazing, initiating, and dumb boy pranks. When the boys were younger I didn't think they needed to know about all that—they just needed to know mom made the final decision and there would be no sleep-away sports camps. MOM card.

Other times, it would have been completely inappropriate to tell the children my reason for saying no. Several times I have had to say, "Hey, you're just going to have to trust me even though you don't understand. You cannot go to that person's house. They are welcome to come here. There will be no more explanation. I'm dropping the MOM card on this one." I don't want my kids in situations where there may be exposure to drugs, alcoholism, pornography, rage, marital anger, or a whole range of other things. If I have some reason to believe one of those things may be present, even if my child's friend is the sweetest, most innocent kid ever, the answer is always no. I'd love to have them come here instead.

I don't allow evil or things that represent evil to come into my house. Movies. Games. Skateboard stickers. You name it. Whatever it is, I will not tolerate anything that even gives a hint of evil. My kids haven't ever tried me on this one, but sometimes a friend will slip up and forget where they are. This is the haven where I invite the Spirit of God to abide. I'll use the MOM card all day long to keep our house clean and honorable to the Lord.

Reaching Their Hearts

Kids need a mom who isn't afraid to be the mom. To say the hard things. Make strong decisions. To discern between wise and harmful choices. To throw down the MOM card is to be the mama bear who loves her cubs with a vengeance. She'll do anything, even be the bad guy, to protect the ones she loves.

Kids Need Their Mom...

To Tell Them What
She'd Do Differently

People say they have no regrets about this life or mistakes they have made. Not me. I have so many. If I am supposed to be pouring truth and wisdom into the hearts of my children, then as it's appropriate, I feel they need to know what I would do differently. And boy, do I have a list.

For starters, I would have learned earlier to sit on the front row at school. Who knows what I was thinking? Maybe I was too shy, or the front row wasn't cool, but kindergarten through grad school, down front is where most of the learning happens. I would have asked questions too. Too afraid to look like I didn't understand, I would sit painfully and wait until someone else asked what I had been dying to know. Even worse, if no one asked, I would keep my question to myself. I spent my entire college career unknown and unseen. The whole thing could have gone differently if I had sat close, introduced myself to my professors, and asked questions, even the uncool ones, when I wanted to know.

Second, and this is painful, I made so many dumb decisions based on appearances, both other people's and my own. A few days ago I told my children, "I am so embarrassed to tell you this, but 25 years ago, when I was single, if a man with thinning hair had passed me on the street I would not have given him a second look. I want you all to know that was one of my all-time dumbest misconceptions ever." My husband has thinning hair, and it grieves me to think one of my children could miss meeting one of the most wonderful people on the planet because of a stupid judgment. I want them to see other people's hearts. To recognize a beautiful countenance. To value a brilliant mind. Other things will change. Hairstyles. Clothing choices. The car they drive. Even teeth—people get new teeth all the time. Oh, the pain of having been a judgmental person. I am so very sorry for that. Maybe if I confess my errors, my kids won't be tempted to make poor judgments of others.

> If our children are going to learn from us, it won't always be from our brilliance.

I also regret my lack of freedom about my own appearance. For years, I never let myself be seen without makeup or styled hair. Needless to say, I think about all the time I spent worrying about my appearance and shake my head with regret. What a burden to carry and a complete waste of time. There are times to pull it all together, and there are times not to concern yourself about appearance. I did not know the difference until later in life. I pray they will learn sooner.

And now, here's where my list kicks into high gear. Before they leave, I am trying to tell my children the things I should have done differently. I should have eaten healthy sooner and made eating choices based on caring for the temple, not on tradition or society. I never should have made fun of people who take vitamins because I should have been taking them earlier. I wish I'd never stopped serious exercise because it's so hard to restart after you're 40. I wish I had learned to walk away from toxic friendships as fast as my feet would take me. I wish I had pursued the more intense graduate degree in my program. I wish I'd listened to my heart and gone on that mission trip to Russia, even though my parents were afraid. I could keep going, like I should have tried avocados sooner, but I think you get the idea. If our children are going to learn from us, it won't always be from our brilliance. Many lessons will come from our regret.

Reaching Their Hearts

Maybe, if we tell our children what we wish we had done differently, they will learn their own lessons of change sooner. I hope they see a mom who is becoming. A mom who is able to learn a new path and then respond. A woman who does things differently because God is growing her up.

When we have regret for past sins, there is a godly sorrow that comes to us. The Bible says that godly sorrow brings repentance. Repentance leads to salvation and a new life without regret (2 Corinthians 7:10). When we have a relationship with Jesus Christ, His forgiveness lets us forget what is behind and strain toward what is ahead (Philippians 3:13-14).

My children probably aren't going to have lives without regret either. But maybe, because of their mom's honesty, they will miss a few things I chose poorly, they will recognize their own mistakes sooner, and most importantly, they will know where to turn with their grief. If they can see Jesus as my Redeemer and friend, I pray they will walk with Him as theirs too.

39

Kids Need Their Mom...

To Make a Big Deal
Out of Grandparents and
Extended Family

"M aMa and PaPa are here!" are some of the sweetest words to ring through our house. The kids run downstairs. There is a lot of hugging and laughing. My parents light up. And you feel the significance of having them here. More family seems to give the children more security and peace. It's the same when Pop and Nana come over. Or the kids' aunt and uncle arrive. My children need their grandparents and extended family to give a generational depth to their lives. As their mom, it's my role to make a big deal out of grandparents and family.

What if our families celebrated the generations instead of focusing on the gap? That celebration and respect should begin in our homes. As a little girl there were various times when our home became a multigeneration home. When my great-grandmother was reaching the end of her life, the back bedroom was fitted with a hospital bed. My mom moved her grandmother into our house so that she could take care of her until her death. Years later, mama moved my grandmother into our house to care for her until a nursing home became the only viable option for her needs.

Through the years my parents had other family members with us from time to time. Every year we were dragged to family reunions where we were squeezed by people we could barely remember. We have been to more funerals and church homecoming services than I can count. And our family made a point to visit relatives most people don't even know they have. My parents made a big deal out of extended family, and I am trying to do the same. I want my children to celebrate their grandparents and embrace their extended family. I want them to value their heritage—they genuinely need to know the people in our family tree. The good, bad, shady, and hilarious. All these people, woven together, create a lineage we'd do well to be acquainted with.

> It's our own quirky, wonderful family, and valuing our family builds into the strong character I desire for my kids.

I am so grateful that in my single-mom years, my children had the great blessing of occasionally being cared for by my parents. When I would be away for a weekend, my parents would move into our house for two nights, bring their dog, Millie, lots of home cooking, and the kind of love only a grandparent can give. The result of those years is that my children know and love their grandparents. They know their likes and dislikes. They see that many of their own traits came from their grandparents, many times saying things like, "Yeah, I inherited my tan skin from PaPa," or "Grayson's artistic gifts came from MaMa." The time they have spent together is an irreplaceable bond that I know God uses to shape and guide them.

This past summer, my parents came with us for a week at the beach. The kids loved having MaMa's great cooking and PaPa's penchant for finding fun things to do, and I think my parents enjoyed seeing the beach through kids' eyes again. There were sand castles to make. Games to play. Ice cream to eat.

One of the sweetest things to happen from my marriage to Scott is the new set of grandparents God has given to the children. Scott's parents, Pop and Nana, have graciously chosen to love us as their own. All of us. They call my children their grandchildren and treat them with such tenderness and joy. I could cry like a baby over their goodness to my children. One day my kids will realize not all stepchildren and grandchildren are received with such extravagant love and devotion. Because of Pop and Nana, I hope my kids' lives will be shaped by the same kind of generosity.

I feel a part of my job is to make a big deal out of our grandparents and family. Their time in our home is supposed to be valuable and honored. Family dinners with grandparents aren't optional—that's what we do. Going to visit them is a high priority. Checking in. Making regular phone calls. Our children need to see their grandparents and our extended families at the top of our priority list. Communicating to them that it's a gift to have family, not just something we do once in a while.

I try to give the grandparents little victories with the kids by giving them inexpensive gift ideas, even when it was my best idea. I want our parents to have the joy of giving my children something they'd love. We opened Facebook accounts for all the grandparents and taught them all how to text. It's cool to have your grandparent care enough to learn your communication language. And it makes the connection with my children easier for our parents to keep.

When my parents come to town, I try to set aside as much of our schedule as possible so they can be our focus. When the schedule won't budge, we try to include them. Grocery store. Soccer games. Chorus concerts. My mom is great at sewing, and even though I could probably figure it out, the kids save all their mending for her. My dad loves cars and milkshakes and driving around town, so the boys know there will be some car talk and milkshakes when PaPa gets here. It's our own quirky, wonderful family, and valuing our family builds into the strong character I desire for my kids.

I do realize that some grandparents and extended family aren't easy to embrace. I'm praying God will give you discernment with the people who are difficult, showing you when to move closer and when to stay away. I hope you can still teach a respect for generations in your home. Even if it may be impossible with your own relatives, introduce your children to other grandparents you know. Teach them to value the wisdom and lives of others. Include multigenerations in your home whenever you can.

Reaching Their Hearts

Our kids need grandparents and extended family. I pray we are all richer because embracing the generations is valued in our homes.

40

Kids Need Their Mom...

To Teach Them How to Keep Their Money Straight, in Order, Facing the Same Direction

My dad was a stickler for orderly money. He kept his change in a dish, and his paper money was always straight, in order by denomination, with all the faces in the same direction. When I was just a little girl, he taught me to do the same. In my family, we were not money wadders with bills stuffed everywhere...we were money sorters with all our bills arranged neat and tidy. As you can imagine, I have given my kids the same instructions about money. Straight, in order, and facing the same direction.

Teaching children this basic system early is the beginning of learning a few simple disciplines in caring for their money. It turns out that when you take care of the bills in your possession, you are also learning how to respect your earnings. When your money is arranged neatly, you know how much you have. And how much you can spend. It's fun to see my kids open their wallets now and peek inside at their neatly arranged bills. They always know exactly what's in there, and I know they are learning to manage what they have been given.

When we married Scott a few years ago, we realized he was a wadder. Ha! It was a hoot to watch the kids, especially AnnaGrace, move in to quickly restore order to his system of currency. He would pull his bills out of his pockets at night and lay the whole mess on his nightstand. AnnaGrace would sneak by sometime later and neatly rearrange his money, straight, in order, and facing the same direction. It's been a few years now, and I think the man has been rehabilitated mainly because AnnaGrace is a hawk and won't let him crumple his money anymore.

More than the basics of order and counting, our children need us to teach and model the use of our money. Here is a simple guideline I learned a long time ago. Its five principles have served me well. I have tried to teach the children with every amount they earn to:

1. Tithe some.

2. Save some.

3. Invest some.

4. Give some.

5. Spend some.

I don't think they need to know amounts, but my kids do need to see me tithing, giving, saving, investing, and paying the bills. Because my business is fairly straightforward, I have had the opportunity to involve the kids in our money matters from very early on. At my speaking events, people buy my books. Many times after going home I have used my little army of children to sort the money. It would have been faster to have an adult do it, but I felt they needed to learn how this world works. I would have one of the kids sorting the cash and another child stamping the backs of checks and putting them in ascending order. After the deposit was all together, I made sure they knew where all that money was going. It was time to pay the bills. First, we had to pay for the books we had sold. Send our taxes to the IRS. Make out a tithe check and begin to pay the bills for our home. Rent. Power. Food.

> My kids needed to know a journey of hard work and planning is required in order to become a financial provider.

It seemed like it would mean more to them to actually touch and sort the money than for me to just tell them what happens. I want them to better understand the chain of events that provides for us. I want them to remember, *Mom sat in that room over there with all kinds of reference books all over the floor. She spent several months typing on the computer and writing and then rewriting the book. One day the shiny new book came to the house, and we had a party to celebrate all that hard work. Mom ordered boxes of books to sell at her events. We loaded them in the car, drove to the church, unloaded the books, and stood there while people paid for books and took them home. The money we brought home pays for the things we need.* Somehow my kids needed to know that a journey of hard work and planning is required in order to become a financial provider. I wanted them to get it. *Oh, all that work produced the income that takes care of our family.*

The whole idea is that one day they will find the thing they love, decide to get all the education they need, and then wisely become a good steward of their gifts and income for themselves and their families.

Very early, my children had to learn that I was not interested in them having what everyone else had, nor would I give in to whining or pouting. You will hear some parents come into a store and tell their children they can have "one thing." Even when I could afford it, I didn't think it was wise to ever tell them they could have "one thing" because most of the time they needed nothing. I wanted the gift of a toy to be a treat, not an entitlement just because they walked politely through a store. As they have been able to earn their own money, the "extras" have come from their spending category.

I have friends who have done much better jobs of training their children to earn money sooner. In my single-mom years, I was in over my head, so adding extra ways for them to earn money didn't connect with my head soon enough. My friends had already established their kids with money-making chores at home and ways to earn money outside the family. I was slower to help my kids, but mainly because I was a crazy person back then. When they were big enough, I did begin paying my children for yard work. Ten dollars for the front yard. Ten for the back. And ten to use the string trimmer and blow. I had been paying a neighborhood friend, so when my boys were able, it seemed like the right thing to let them earn the money. The first two have had part-time jobs at bistros and yogurt shops. My next son is 15 and so very ready to find his first summer job and the paycheck that comes with it.

Reaching Their Hearts

The financial lessons that we begin early with our children will be the lessons that shape their earning and spending for a lifetime. Let them learn by organizing the dollars in your wallet. Help them see how money is earned and where it has to go before there is a treat.

41

Kids Need Their Mom...

To Be Patient About Things like Thumb-Sucking and Pacifiers

When AnnaGrace was born, the doctor handed me that precious baby, and in just a matter of minutes, she had worked her tiny newborn hand up to her mouth, and right before my very eyes, my little babygirl began sucking her thumb. I was amazed. None of my other three had come from the womb sucking their thumb, but the nurses said little AnnaGrace had probably been sucking her thumb for months in utero.

Well, I was the mom of three previous pacifier babies, so I was sure I could break this newborn of her thumb obsession. As soon as I could locate a pacifier in the hospital, my mission began. Transition this baby to a pacifier so that in time I could take the pacifier away. So that in time this child would not need expensive orthodontia. Weeks went by, and multiple times a day I ever so gently moved her little hand and replaced her thumb with a fancy, pediatric-approved pacifier. And every single time, the same thing happened. *Suck. Suck. Suck. A moment of consideration. Pacifier rejected. Thumb. Ahhh.* I could not believe that this fourth child of mine was going to beat me. But she did. Her commitment to thumb-sucking never wavered, and my determination to change her mind eventually gave out. The new baby won. We had ourselves a thumb-sucker.

After being forced to accept a thumb-sucking child, I did eventually come to embrace her affliction as a gift. First, I did not have to buy any more pacifiers, ever, although her older brother relapsed and took every pink pacifier we had received at baby showers, hid them under his bed, and secretly retrieved them under the cover of night. One night I walked in to find him in the dark, sucking away on a big pink pacifier. "William, you already gave those up months ago," I said as I took that pink pacifier and put it into the pocket of my robe. Brilliant even back then, that kid reached down under his blanket and produced another pink pacifier, and with the happiest brown eyes you've ever seen, he plopped that thing right into his mouth. The boy had a stash. I'm still praying that I did not cause some kind of emotional trauma when I took his collection.

Now, all this time later, each one of my kids has had years and years of orthodontia. What in the world was I so worried about? Oh, how I regret being uptight about too many little things when they were little. Why did I worry so much about appearances and buckteeth and what other people's children were doing? For goodness' sake, uptight has been the embarrassment of my mothering.

> Sometimes our kids need patience and understanding a whole lot more than they need to abide by the parenting books.

I wanted to be the best, most conscientious, most organized mom ever. All wonderful and noble aspirations until the overwhelming stress of self-imposed expectations begins to eat your lunch. And your spirit. And even your joy. I thought I could pack the best diaper bag ever checked in at the church nursery, and I'm sure I did for the first couple of children. By the fourth baby, the stress of it all had kicked in, most of my pretense was gone, and the nursery was lucky if I wrote her name on a diaper and tossed it over when I signed her in. I tried so hard to keep hair bows perfectly poised in my first daughter's hair. By the last child, I had realized two-year-olds don't like hair bows and that's okay. Slowly and painfully, God taught me that there is a difference between what my kids needed and the illusion I was trying to paint. Learning to embrace my thumb-sucking, bucktooth child without any judgment was such a sweet place of freedom for both of us. The uptight mom needed to chill about some things. And my innocent little pumpkin needed to be released from the ridiculous stress I had made.

By the time AnnaGrace was eight years old, she was still sucking her thumb and had the teeth to prove it. By that time, she sucked only at night or if she was tired or maybe if she was hungry. She knew she needed to stop, but oh, how hard it was to break a habit that began before she was born!

We went to see the orthodontist, and he told her he could permanently put an appliance in the top of her mouth that would break the suction, and eventually she would stop sucking her thumb. He told her he would give her three months to stop on her own. That night in bed she cried and cried, trying to make herself stop but truly not being able to. I snuggled up beside her. "Does it feel good to suck your thumb, baby?"

"Oh, yes, mama, it really does. It's peaceful," she replied.

"Well, then, here's what I think. Just suck that thumb all you can for the next three months. You're going to have braces either way. Might as well get all the peace you can."

I'm happy to report that her braces are cute as can be. Her teeth are just about finished straightening. And this uptight mom wasted a lot of energy proving nothing. Sometimes our kids need patience and understanding a whole lot more than they need to abide by the parenting books. I regret not letting William keep those pacifiers a little longer. He was only 20 months old. Poor little kid.

Reaching Their Hearts

As moms, I think we're supposed to receive the beautiful wisdom of the moms who have gone before us and the childcare professionals who have expert knowledge. We need to consider each one of our children individually. Pray to God for direction. Then, after taking a deep breath, lay down our own ridiculous expectations, insecurities, and striving.

Now, whenever I meet a little child with buckteeth, I smile to myself and think about how much they must love sucking their thumb. Then in my head, I applaud that mom who probably learned much sooner than me, you can straighten teeth. Sometimes, the comfort of your child matters more.

Kids Need Their Mom...

To Let Them Make Really Dumb Mistakes Without Condemnation

My kids have made several dumb mistakes. The kinds of things that made me want to cry and fume and stomp through the house. Actually, I think I did cry and fume and stomp a few times. They were the kind of dumb mistakes that make you want to yell into their face, "What in the world were you thinking? You, of all people, know better."

And they do know better, all of them. All of my kids know right from wrong. They have each one asked Jesus Christ to be their Savior. They have attended church, youth groups, Bible studies, and Christian school. They have a Bible teacher for a mom. For crying out loud, my kids know the right thing to do. And they have also been taught that when they do not know what to do, if they are unsure or confused or feeling pressured, do nothing! Stand still and call your mom. Or run and call your mom. Either way, do not choose out of confusion or pressure.

Yet, we've had some dumb mistakes and the consequences that come attached to dumb mistakes. And I hate it. Doggone it, I just hate for them to have to suffer a stupid consequence that could have been avoided. But my four children are certifiable sinners. Each born with a sin nature. Each parented by this mom who every day keeps on proving how much she needs a Savior too. And it looks like none of us will be able to raise children without suffering through a few, or many, dumb mistakes. So given that discouraging news, the question becomes, how will we love them when they've really blown it?

First thing, I believe we have permission to be mad. Sure, I think we are supposed to feel a righteous anger over the poor choices our kids have made. But the Bible instructs us to be angry and sin not. What that means is that we can feel the anger, and talk about our anger, and pray through our anger, but not one of us should make a decision based on our anger. I know that our Father God in heaven has surely been angry over the disobedience of His people, but oh, praise Him, He has not dealt with us according to His anger. Our Father in heaven disciplines us from His love. As parents of disobedient kids, we are called to do the same.

> Let them learn from their consequences sooner because the consequences they will suffer as adults are so much more painful.

Second, if your child has blown it big, you have to let the consequences unfold. Hard as it may be to watch, the worst possible thing you can do is to stop what is unfortunately deserved. For some of my mom friends, that has meant watching their child be kicked out of school because that really good kid who knew better chose video games over attending class. For some it's meant a trip to the police station or visits to the jail. Rehabs. Drug centers. AA meetings. Consequences are awful and especially when they belong to our children.

Several years ago, I met a mom with four children. She had two, and then ten years went by and two more. She said she had learned so much raising the first two. The second pair of children were really benefiting from the lessons. I asked her, "What is the biggest piece of advice you can give to me from all you have learned?" She said, "I learned the hard way not to save them." She went on to explain that with her first children, very early, she thought she had to save them from their consequences. If they left a backpack at home, she would get back in the car and run it to them. If they forgot their homework, she'd make an excuse for their forgetfulness and ask the teacher for an extension. She told me that saving them early produced two grown children who do not know how to take care of themselves. She wishes she had let them learn from their consequences sooner because the consequences they are suffering as adults are so much more painful.

That lady's words really made an impression on me. As hard as it is to let my kid take a zero because they left their paper at home, I have learned to do it. They've had to sit out games because of forgotten uniforms. I remember one day in Taylor's fourth grade. The kids were allowed to wear shorts to school, but they had to be within the dress code, not too short. That morning I told Taylor I thought her shorts were too short. She disagreed with a thousand words to tell me why she was right. I let her wear them to school. Later that day, I had to call the school office for a completely different reason. The secretary said, "Just so you know, Taylor's shorts were too short today, but we're going to let it slide because it's her first offense." I responded to the secretary, "Do you mind not letting it slide? I don't want Taylor to think she can bend the rules." When I picked her up later that day, she came to the car, tugging at those shorts, trying to make them longer. I smiled to myself. The tiniest little voice confessed that she had been called to the principal's office because her shorts were too short.

Finally, the consequence is enough. We are supposed to discuss the dumb mistake or the flat-out sin. Talk through the consequence and then adhere to whatever discipline is required. And then, you and I need to be the first to forgive their disobedience or their disappointing behavior. After it's all said and done, we have to let the consequence be enough. It is wrong to keep reminding them of their sin. It is belittling to continue to hold their mistake against them, like an accountant keeps a ledger of credits and debits. With your forgiveness, the slate needs to be wiped clean. In your heart, in your words, with your tone, and with your affection, you and I must teach our children what the grace of forgiveness feels like.

Reaching Their Hearts

Our kids will do some really dumb things in this life, but like Christ, may we be the first to give them no condemnation.

Kids Need Their Mom...

To Introduce Them to
Her Friend Named Jesus

I f we don't do anything else on this earth, introducing our children to personal faith in Jesus is the single-most life-changing, power-giving thing you and I can do. Here's what I believe. I may blow it as a mom. I might make mistakes that cause my children pain or heartache or unintentionally influence them wrongly, but if my child has a genuine relationship with the Savior of the world, Jesus Christ, then Christ in them will be Healer, Redeemer, Savior, Counselor, and Friend.

And so, let's begin with the obvious. We cannot impart what we do not possess. You and I cannot introduce our children to Jesus if we do not know Him for ourselves. But I also want you to know it's never too late with God. No matter how old your children are, or how far away from God you have been, I want you to know that God is wildly and eternally in love with you. He wants a relationship with you today. I want to tell you about my girlfriend Carlye.

Carlye did not become a follower of Jesus until her youngest son, Dace, was ten years old. She had grown up in a home where she had attended church sometimes. Her parents talked about God occasionally. But Carlye had never made a decision to investigate Christianity or attend church regularly. She just wasn't interested. Married with two children, Carlye and her family sat in her living room one afternoon with her grown-up nephew Gary. Gary had come for a visit and began to explain to Carlye the principles of Christianity. Gary said something like this:

Our God, the God whom we worship, is the Creator of all things. In the beginning, God created this world, including a man named Adam and a woman named Eve. Adam and Eve chose to disobey God. When they disobeyed, sin and evil entered this world. At that point, God could have chosen to leave His sinful, disobedient creation, but He did not. Since the first sin, the story of the Bible is the story of God's love and His gracious plan to redeem the sinner and restore His relationship with His creation. From His great love, God sent His son, Jesus, to this earth for that very reason, to redeem the sinner and restore our relationship with God.

The Bible says Jesus died on the cross to pay the punishment we deserved. His life paid for our sin. The Bible also says that anyone who believes Jesus is the Son of God can call Him Savior. He is our Savior because He saves us from the punishment we deserve.

When you decide to follow Jesus, the Bible promises several things. First, you are forgiven of your sins, today and for all eternity. Second, every person who believes in Jesus will spend eternity with Him in heaven. Third, the Holy Spirit comes to live inside the soul of every believer to give wisdom, guidance, and comfort. And fourth, not only will you be with God in heaven, His son, Jesus, will be your friend here on this earth. He will be with you always. You will never be alone again.

As the story goes, after Gary had finished explaining the importance of Jesus and a life spent following him, he turned to Carlye and asked, "Carlye, do you want to become a follower of Jesus Christ?" Carlye says she knew everything Gary had explained was true, but she looked over at her ten-year-old son, Dace, who'd been listening to the whole conversation. Dace looked at his mom, and with all the enthusiasm in the world he said, "Come on, mom, go for it!"

> God does not make it tricky for anyone to follow Him. You can ask Jesus Christ to be your Savior with a simple prayer.

I love that. I love that Dace watched his mom give her life to Jesus. And I love that right after his mom, Dace asked Jesus to be his Savior too.

Maybe today you are reading these pages and realize that you have never made a decision to follow Jesus Christ. I want you to know there are no hoops to jump through. God does not make it tricky for anyone to follow Him. You can ask Jesus Christ to be your Savior with a simple prayer like this:

> *Jesus, I believe You are the Son of God. I believe You died to pay for the punishment I deserve. Will You forgive me of my sins and make me Yours? I want to follow You with my life and live according to the truths in the Bible. Amen.*

The Bible instructs us to meet with other believers for the purposes of worship, fellowship, and instruction. I'd encourage you to find a church in your area where they believe in Jesus and follow the teachings of the Bible. Then go to church and become a part of God's family in your town. Meet with them. Pray with them. Serve alongside them. And show your children how to do the same.

Maybe you have been hesitant about your faith or distant from God. Can I encourage you to make your relationship with God the first priority of your life? Everything you need to become an amazing mom will be provided to you through the power and wisdom of the Holy Spirit. The most important relationship your child will ever have is a passionate, vibrant relationship with the Savior of the world. And who better to introduce them to Jesus than you?

Reaching Their Hearts

We give our children the sweetest blessing when we first follow Jesus with our own lives and then help them to follow Jesus with theirs.

In the words of a passionate, ten-year-old boy, "Come on, mom, go for it!"

$$\left(\,44\,\right)$$

Kids Need Their Mom...

To Set the Tone for the Family

Currently, my husband and I live in a house with three teenagers, ages 13 to 17. Our 20-year-old is away at school, but we still count her in the same category, only one year past teen. This morning before school, not one of my children came downstairs singing a song, dancing through the kitchen, or kissing and hugging their mom. That's just not where they are right now and especially not in the mornings.

Every one of my children dragged themselves down at the last possible minute. All of them forgot at least three things, and each time had to lug themselves back up the stairs for the forgotten items. They barely spoke even the slightest painful morning syllables. They had on the wrong coats for the obvious snow falling outside, and oh, the misery each one had to suffer in taking off their jacket to put on a heavier coat. They could barely open their mouths to put in morsels of breakfast, as though each bite were so heavy their arm might surely break. Ten

> On behalf of the people I love, who cannot yet think clearly for themselves, I am choosing joy!

minutes past time to go, they piled on the backpacks, gathered their gym bags, took the rest of their uneaten breakfast, and somehow made it out to the car so they could fall back asleep while they were luxuriously driven to school in a heated car with soft music. It's the cushy life, I tell you.

If my teenage children were allowed to set the tone for our home, we'd be a bunch of droopy-eyed, slow-moving, barely thinking, ever-forgetful, lethargic, disinterested poops. That is, until some time after dinner, when their little minds come alive and they can then talk nonstop, take a four-mile run, shoot baskets until I force them to stop keeping the neighbors awake, and find a hundred things to do except go to bed on time. But here's the deal—I decided a long time ago that my kids don't set the tone for our home. I do. My husband does. But not the moody, hormonal, sluggish, yet-to-be consistent people.

Sometimes moms forget that we are in charge! We set the tone. We chart the course. We turn the ship, even though slowly some days. I wake up happy. Really. Just flat-out happy, ready to talk, excited to be here. Finally, I have realized that morning happiness can be obnoxious to the slow-waking, so I have tried to tone it down a bit through the years. But doggone it, I refuse to let the barely breathing rule my house or set the tone for my family. Even if I am in the minority some days, I'm still in charge of this thing, and on behalf of the people I love, who cannot yet think clearly for themselves, I am choosing joy!

I choose joy in the mornings. And after school. And when they have friends over. And at their ball games. And in the hallways at church. And when I'm pulling in at carpool. I love to call them sweet nicknames, of which I have hundreds, so I do. I love to kiss them and hug them, so I do. I honk the horn and wave like I mean it. Eye-rolling does not dissuade me. Unreturned hugs on the sidewalk at school do not discourage me. I just try to keep in mind that they are little dorks who have no idea what a blessing it is to have a mama who is wildly in love with them, and their little insecurities will not keep me from loving them, sometimes loudly, with great joy and enthusiasm.

This morning I greeted all the sleepyheads with smiles and hugs and kisses. I threw in a little dancing before they left just so they'd smile on the inside even though their stubborn morning fog refused to let their faces give in on the outside. I don't know if anyone is keeping score, but one thing I know for sure, I'm winning on this one. I love my kids, but they don't run this place. They are allowed to move slowly and act sleepy and generally approach life like a teenager, but I will not allow the beautiful spirit of our home to be diminished on the days when they "don't feel it."

Kids need their moms to set the tone. They need us to be consistent in countenance, especially because their developing bodies and minds are not. What better way to teach them about a spirit of joy than to weave that attribute through even the most mundane parts of our routine. To wake them with a tender joy, no matter what disappointment you may have felt the night before. To give them a joyful "do over" every single morning. To respond to them with a joyful tone. To begin our conversations with kindness and patience.

There is a powerful teaching I think we'd all do well to practice. It's the idea of "taking no offense." Too many people in this world are too easily offended. They react from their offense. Sometimes enjoy their offense. And many even live every single day as the perpetually offended. Choosing to set the tone of joy for my home means that many days I consciously choose not to be offended by my family, by their lack of enthusiasm, or even by their immature forgetfulness. To take no offense means that I am choosing to live higher and brighter than the fog of a teenage mind. Taking no offense means remembering that I am the mom. They are the growing who need to be nurtured, instructed, and shown.

Reaching Their Hearts

Today, if you decided to set the tone for your family, what one thing would you change? What one thing would you add? What adjustment would you make in your own heart?

Let's be moms who create an atmosphere of joy for our families. The tone is ours to set. Ready, set, shine!

45

Kids Need Their Mom...

To Teach Them to Genuinely Respect All People, Cultures, Denominations, and Creeds

William was about nine years old. My friend had taken him with her son to his first soccer practice with his new soccer team. As the story has been told to me, after he got to the field, William met a little boy named Ethan. Ethan's mom was there watching and later told me what happened after William and Ethan began kicking the soccer ball together.

Evidently Ethan had encountered some boys at his school who had ridiculed him for being Jewish. The week before they had gotten him in a corner at a party and told him he was going to hell. Understandably, Ethan was hesitant to make a new friend that day. He and William were kicking the ball when Ethan decided to put all his chips on the table. Ethan boldly said to William, "Hey, you need to know I'm Jewish." Ethan's mom told me that without missing a kick, William looked up and shrugged, "So? Jesus was a Jew." The boys ran off kicking the ball together, and she thought to herself, *I want to meet that boy's mom. Most little boys have no idea that Jesus was Jewish. Someone has taught that boy well.*

William and Ethan went on to become the best of friends after that day. William later attended Ethan's bar mitzvah. Ethan and his family came to our wedding a few years ago. As William's mom, I was grateful, and relieved, to hear about William's response to Ethan. Whew. You know, you think you teach them right, and you pray that you have given them a respect for others, but what a blessing when you realize it's taken hold in their souls.

Kids need their moms to teach them how to respect all people. Each one of us, though we may be incredibly different, is made in the image of God and loved by God. I pray that we are teaching our children to see others as God does. To love people of different cultures. To build friendships with others not like us.

I want my children to be thinking people who are educated in their faith and the tenants of Scripture. I want them to know what they believe and why our family is a Christian family. But I do not want them to be smart about their faith so that they can use that knowledge to judge someone else or to berate the faith of others. I desire knowledge for them so that they might be steadfast in their understanding. So that they can love others from a place of wisdom instead of judging others from a posture of insecurity.

> God has brought into our lives so many interesting people that we may have otherwise missed.

To respect others does not mean that we always agree with them, but I want my children to learn to respect the person and then disagree graciously. My oldest son is a junior in high school and having great conversations with his science teacher concerning evolution versus creation. Just the other day after a long lecture, Grayson said he raised his hand and said to his teacher, "Sir, I don't mean to be argumentative, but what you just presented to us makes no sense at all." I said, "Grayson, were you respectful?" "Yes, mom," he assured me. Evidently he was, because the teacher Grayson keeps disagreeing with recommended to the principal that Grayson be chosen as a student ambassador to represent his high school.

A few years ago when we moved to Greensboro, North Carolina, I didn't realize we were moving to such a culturally diverse city, but we were. Greensboro has through the years been a center of relocation for refugees from all over the world, and many of those refugees have made Greensboro their home. On the main street that runs near our house, there are over 50 varieties of ethnic markets where you can find the foods or goods common to one particular country. I've made it my goal to shop in all of them. Sometimes we go into places and I have no idea what language is being spoken or what country the folks originate from, but we are learning! God has brought into our lives so many interesting people that we may have otherwise missed if we had chosen to shop only where people who look like us shop. The kids beg me to take them to the African hair-braiding shop around the corner from our house. One day, I'm sure I'll work up my nerve to go in for a braid or two.

We do not have to be insecure concerning other denominations or creeds when we have a solid understanding of our own faith. I have never known of anyone who became a follower of Christ because they were judged or hated. Every single person I know who comes to Christ does so because of love and friendship.

I am committed to the work of an organization called World Vision. World Vision was founded by Bob Pierce and based on these words: "May our hearts be broken with the things that break the heart of God." If we keep that same heart concerning every interaction and every relationship, God is able to give us a grace and a respect for every kind of people in every kind of situation. If we have a heart like God's, then we have a heart that sees past the color of skin. A heart that breaks over the chains of sin. A heart that desires to provide for the needy and to rescue the afflicted.

Reaching Their Hearts

May our children see in us women who genuinely respect all people and love them with the same love that has been given to us by God. And then, by the grace of God, may our kids multiply that respect into all the generations to come after us.

46

Kids Need Their Mom...

To Teach the Boys
How to Love a Wife

William must have been six years old. He walked into the kitchen where I was getting ready to bake. Out from the pantry I lugged the big KitchenAid mixer, set it on the counter, and then began locating the rest of my ingredients.

"Mom," he asked, "did that thing cost a lot of money?"

"The mixer?" I realized what he was admiring. "Well, yes, honey, that's a fancy mixer, and it's really expensive. MaMa and PaPa gave it to me one year as a Christmas present."

He just kept standing there with his little mind calculating. "Yep, I'm gonna have to buy my wife one of those one day."

"That's right, baby," I told him, grinning to myself. "I'm sure she'll love to have one."

I loved that at six, he was already thinking about how to provide for his wife. But the truth is, our boys need every one of these years with us to learn how to love their wives well. It's a very fabulous thing if they can learn that from their dad too, but many times that is not the case. As moms, we have so much to teach our boys about how to treat a woman. How to love her and care for her. How to listen and respond to her. How to enjoy what is shared and laugh at the differences. So much of how they will treat their wives comes from how we have taught them to treat us.

In trying to prepare my two sons to love their wives well, I am intentional about teaching them how to interact with me. Even now in their teenage years, where it would be easy for them to pull away, I keep moving toward them, trying to keep the communication going and desiring to use these last years at home building character that will be the strong foundation of a healthy marriage and family.

I really try to draw the boys into discussions with their sisters and me. One of the most powerful things they can learn is how to have a conversation with a woman, embracing her femininity and her unique personality, learning to see her gifts, and never belittling her weaknesses. A part of learning how to have a conversation is learning how to disagree respectfully. My boys are not allowed to speak rudely with me, nor do I let them mumble, walk off, pout, or say disrespectful things. I feel like one of the keys to respectful conversation is never allowing them to do otherwise.

> I want them to value the "girly" in their wives and bless her.

I have taken my boys with me everywhere. The have probably been to more women's conferences than any man should have to attend. Usually they sit in the back and feign attention, but I do know they have absorbed so much just from all the interactions. They go with me to buy furniture, to buy baby gifts, to get groceries, to choose new candles. I have forced them to get out of the car, interact with things that concern our home, and then, even if it kills them, give me some kind of opinion. I make them help us get the house ready for a party by hanging the streamers, bringing chairs in from the garage, and putting the tablecloths on the table. I don't want them to perceive "girly" things as goofy or inferior. Even though they may never be interested in any of those things, I want them to value the "girly" in their wives and bless her instead of resent her or demean her interests. Oh, how I pray they will show enthusiasm over the things she's excited about because I forced them to engage all these years!

Continuing to hug and snuggle our boys, even holding hands for half a second, is a little premarriage training for the tender affection his wife will crave. She will long for my son to hold her hand when they walk, and put his arm around her to hold her close. I work on getting a laugh out of the boys every time I can. It keeps them remembering how to laugh out loud, and laughter with their wives will be such a key piece of loving them well.

Last week, our older son, Grayson, asked a sweet little girl to prom. After he told us the whole story of having asked her, I said, "Baby, you're going to have to re-ask her."

"Huh? What do you mean?" he asked.

"Well, Grayson, it sounds like you sat her down and asked her to go with you and gave her a big long speech about just going as friends," I started.

"I did. I just want us to have a good time, and I didn't want it to be weird," he defended.

"I understand, but, honey, it's prom! It's one of the few proms she will attend in her lifetime. You just about ripped all the joy right out of it by making it a business deal. You're going to have to go back and ask her again, but this time, it needs to be fun. A pizza with pepperoni that spells PROM? A scavenger hunt? Something better."

"Gosh, mom, I don't know these things."

"That's why you have me."

I want my sons to love their wives with fun and special plans, remembering that it's fun to make the one you love feel special. A little silliness now and then can make a tough season so much lighter.

All of their growing up years, I have begun many conversations with my boys, "When you are a husband…" and then I'll fill in the blank:

> Bring her flowers as often as you can.
>
> Ask to be forgiven first.
>
> Own your faults before you look for hers.
>
> Ask God what to do and how to respond before you say a word.
>
> Hold the door. Stand when she comes to the table. Help her with her coat.
>
> Dance even if you feel goofy.
>
> Lavish her with kind words…everybody needs encouragement.
>
> Find out what makes her laugh. Do that a lot.
>
> Share as many things as you can. Meals. Chores. Hobbies.
>
> Never belittle her for things she couldn't control. The parents she has. The place she grew up. The things she's never done.

Reaching Their Hearts

Oh how I pray that our boys will love their wives with an amazing, life-giving, encouraging love. May that love training begin here and now, intentionally passing from us to them.

47

Kids Need Their Mom...

To Teach the Girls
How to Love a Husband

Oh my goodness, has the Lord taken me on a journey about this one! I was married for about 14 years, lived 7 as a single mom, and today, I have been remarried for almost 3 years. And oh, how I desperately long for my two daughters to know how to love their husband well. My first line of training is to teach them by loving their stepdad like a crazy woman right in front of their eyes. As married moms, we are teaching our daughters all day long how to love a husband.

Scott and I have the privilege of enjoying one another in front of the kids. We kiss and hug hello, walk each other to the car, giggle in the kitchen, and truly like being together. I'll ride with him to the store or hop in the car to pick up kids at soccer just to get a few more minutes to talk to him in our day. I want my daughters to see their mom enjoying her husband because I pray they too will demonstrate in tone, expression, and words, their great joy over their husband.

I am so very grateful for the amazing husband and dad that Scott is to us. He's just a good guy, all day long, every single day. As far as we can figure out, the man has only two flaws: he misplaces his keys and he hangs up the phone like he's running to put out a fire. Even if I do spot another flaw one day, I have made it my vow to never, ever speak poorly of Scott to anyone and especially to the children. We laugh about the keys and the quick way he gets off the phone, and I tell the children, "He needs us!"

We should major on our husbands' strengths and minimize their flaws.

Every time I can give Scott respect, I try to do that, especially in front of the children. First, respect speaks to him. It's one of the ways I try to love him well. And second, the children need to hear what genuine respect sounds like. Feel what it feels like. See what respect does in the soul of the receiver. They also need to live in a house where they see their mom loving her husband with encouragement. I send Scott out the door every morning with a "Go get 'em, honey! You are the man!" I pay attention to his golf scores and the ball games that he cares about, and the man rarely comes downstairs without me saying, "You are the cutest thing!" The girls watch him light up, and I pray they use the same kind of encouragement to love their husbands too.

> The man rarely comes downstairs without me saying, "You are the cutest thing!" The girls watch him light up, and I pray they use the same kind of encouragement to love their husbands too.

One of the sweetest gifts we give to our husbands is to accept where they are today. If his load is heavy, offering to stand under it with him instead of condemning. If everything is falling apart, getting in there to help pick up the pieces. If he's sick, caring for him. Worried, praying with him. Let's ask God to do the work of change in their hearts and learn to approach our marriage relationships with acceptance instead of judgment. In this world where it's very cool to point out what everyone does wrong or the mistakes they have made, may we love our husbands with a gracious understanding that they are men in process. Forgiven sinners. People still growing. Human beings to be loved and cherished. I think my girls feel my complete acceptance of Scott. I don't moan about the things that don't matter. I let him get around to things as he is able. He is a very smart man with a beautiful mother. I am his wife, here to love, respect, and share this sweet journey of marriage.

A word to the single moms, because I have been you. First, make sure to drop all the ex-husband bashing with your children. If you have to talk it out, please see a counselor or talk to a girlfriend, but you have to discontinue all that kind of conversation around the kids for two reasons. First, you keep reopening the wound for them. And deepening the wound. Let them heal. Please, have mercy, and let them heal. And second, you are teaching your children more about condemnation and bitterness than you realize. Your ex-husband may not be the kind of man you want your daughter to marry, but speak to her positively about how to love instead of feeding her years of negativity and hurt. Maybe you can begin a conversation like this:

> *Honey, after all we've been through, I bet you are learning so much about how to have a good marriage and how to love your future husband. Tell me about some of the great ways you want to build love in your family...*

Reaching Their Hearts

As with almost everything in mothering, teaching our daughters to love their husbands is a classroom requiring about 20 years of instruction. Let her see you love well and when you have not, let her see your repentance, your change, and your growth.

48

To Identify the Characteristics of a Fool and Tell Them What to Do When They Meet One

I was born naïve and raised naïve. That's nothing to be proud of, but it's just the way I was raised. My parents did not teach me to be suspicious of people, and honestly, I grew up believing most people told the truth. That's all fine and good until you realize that the rest of this world did not get the same life instructions. Never having any reason to mistrust or doubt, I am still to this day taken aback when I encounter people who invent lies full of deception.

I wish that someone had sat me down when I was a little girl and said, "Honey, there are some people in this world who look like you and sound like you and work like you, but they are not the real thing. There are imposters and tricksters and slick people who will turn your head inside out and make you feel like a crazy person." Then it would have been great if they had handed me a tip sheet so I could have known what to look for. Unfortunately, I have learned about these people in the hardest possible ways. It turns out, though, that the Bible spoke of these people long before I ever met one. The Bible calls these crazy-makers fools, and the book of Proverbs contains a tip sheet so you'll know how to spot one.

Even as I'm writing this, I'm realizing that I probably need to pull out every passage of Scripture concerning fools, choose a few by categories, and then spend several weeks going over these with the kids. If our children can learn to distinguish as the Bible directs, all kinds of heartache will be avoided, not to mention the wisdom that will be gained.

The book of Proverbs lists the following as the characteristics of a fool:

- *The fool is unrighteous.* The fool hates what is holy, and sin is like a sport to him. "Fools mock at sin, but among the upright there is good will" (14:9 NASB).

- *The fool is unwise.* Unwise means fools do not possess wisdom, nor are they able to obtain it. I have heard this spoken about the unwise fool: "You don't get it that you don't get it." From their own arrogance, fools do not even understand they are lacking. "Do not speak in the hearing of a fool, for he will despise the wisdom of your words" (23:9 NASB).

- *The fool is unrealistic.* Fools cannot see things as they really are. They overestimate themselves, act with pride, and are always waiting for their "ship to come in." "Wisdom is in the presence of the one who has understanding, but the eyes of a fool are on the ends of the earth" (17:24 NASB).

- *The fool is undisciplined.* Every area of a fool's life lacks discipline because she regards self-control as needless. She is undisciplined with her money, her temper, and her mouth. "The tongue of the wise makes knowledge acceptable, but the mouth of fools spouts folly" (15:2 NASB).

- *The fool is unreliable.* Fools cannot keep their word and their words should always be questioned. They are dishonest in their work and cannot be trusted. "Like an archer who wounds everyone, so is he who hires a fool or who hires those who pass by" (26:10 NASB).

- *The fool is unteachable.* Fools reject wisdom and instruction, and to attempt to instruct a fool is a waste of time. "The fear of the LORD is the beginning of knowledge; fools despise wisdom and instruction" (1:7 NASB).

- *The fool is unliked.* This person brings strife, confusion, and grief. "Drive out the scoffer, and contention will go out, even strife and dishonor will cease" (22:10 NASB).

There are foolish people in this world, and the sooner our children learn how to recognize their characteristics, the sooner they can respond with wisdom to these people in their lives. The book of Proverbs is also very clear about what we are supposed to do:

- *Avoid them.* "Leave the presence of a fool, or you will not discern words of knowledge" (14:7 NASB).

- *Don't waste your time on a fool.* "Do not speak in the hearing of a fool, for he will despise the wisdom of your words" (23:9 NASB).

- *Do not let fools drag you down to their level.* A real-life application might be, don't date a fool. Don't marry a fool. Don't go into business with a fool. "Do not answer a fool according to his folly, or you will also be like him" (26:4 NASB).

- *Do not give respect to a fool.* "Like snow in summer and like rain in harvest, so honor is not fitting for a fool" (26:1 NASB).

Finally, we instruct our children about the reality of foolish people among us, one, so that they will learn to respond with wisdom, and two, so that they do not become one.

Things are so much different now than when I was growing up. Evil abounds and foolishness is at every turn. I want my kids to be armed with the truths of Scripture, and then I want them to hear the words of their mom echoing in their heads, "Baby, when you think you have encountered a fool, run. Go to the other side of the street. Sit on the other side of the room. Do not give that person your phone number. Do not waste your time on building a relationship with them. RUN."

> I want my kids to be armed with the truths of Scripture.

The good news is that not even the fool lives outside the realm of God's faithfulness. The most foolish among us can be redeemed by the miraculous power of God. But until that happens and the change is sustained, our children would do well to avoid all contact and entanglement. I don't think God would have spent so much time in the Bible giving us lists of characteristics of fools if He didn't mean for us to take their presence seriously.

Reaching Their Hearts

We have to teach our children how to recognize these tragic individuals and give them permission to run like the wind!

49

Kids Need Their Mom...

To Train Them to Listen to Her

Moms really do know a thing or two. We all want our children to listen to us. From the time they are toddlers, listening and obeying are two of the primary tasks of our parenting instruction. In our house, not listening to me was never an option. With intentional clarity, I would say to my child, "Look at mama," and then I would give a clear and deliberate instruction with a tone that meant, *You have no options right now. You must listen and obey.* With eye-to-eye contact, the kids learned early to listen and respond, mainly because I used "Look at me" only for something important or protective.

Eventually, they outgrew "Look at me" as a listening prompt, even though eye-to-eye contact continued as a valuable tool. As preteens and teenagers, training them to listen to me has been an exercise in building trust. There are several things I have tried to be aware of through the years:

1. What I say to them must be trustworthy so that they do not learn to tune out—"Oh, mom, she just says all that stuff, but it's not really true."

2. When I make a promise to them, then I must keep it or intentionally come back to them and reissue the promise on new terms. "Baby, I know that I promised we'd get new cleats this week, but our schedule became crazy. How about we go Saturday afternoon?"

3. I cannot use my words or my knowledge to exasperate my children. A conversation with them is not a throw-down of how smart I am compared to how little they know. To exasperate my child is discouraging. I turn off discouraging people, and they will too.

4. With my boys, I begin a conversation with them using brief, concise thoughts. They respond to brevity and little bites of information with greater interest.

5. With my girls, I begin a conversation filled with all the frills and details I think they'd like to have. They perk up and listen because it's the kind of conversation they are interested in.

6. With all my children, I have used the power of story to teach them to listen. If I can weave a good tale and throw in some humor, my kids will usually hang with me, anticipating a good punch line or take-away.

We teach our children to listen to us because they have learned that they can trust what we say. Many times through the years, I have set up a situation with one of my children just for the purpose of building trust. Maybe I'll encourage them to try out for an opportunity I already know they are qualified for. Or I'll give them an instruction that leads to a little victory I have prearranged. Maybe my next door neighbor told me they were looking for someone to care for their dog, so later that afternoon I'd say to one of the children, "You've been looking for some extra spending money. Why don't you go next door and ask the neighbors if there is anything you can do to earn a little money?"

> Great listeners gather wisdom, insight, and discernment.

I am praying my children will come to understand that listening to me will usually have a payoff. Our conversation will be interesting. I'm going to ask them good questions and really try to understand their hearts. There may be a punch line that's fun or a take-away that's moving. I'm not going to waste their precious listening by indulging in gossip or ranting or selfishness. And in their listening, they can trust that any wisdom that has come to me will be transferred as clearly and directly as I am able.

Learning to listen to their mom is a life skill that will multiply dividends in our children's future relationships, careers, and families. Listening well is also a characteristic of godliness: "My dear brothers and sisters, take note of this: Everyone should be quick to listen, slow to speak and slow to become angry" (James 1:19).

Many times a day in this world, we have to listen to someone, even though we lack the want-to. For adults, to possess the skill of listening anyway is invaluable. We begin teaching our kids to listen when they'd rather do something else in the earliest years of "Look at me."

To be able to truly listen to someone is a gift that you give to your child's future spouse. Husband or wife, they will thank you for teaching your child the art of listening. The most successful business people in the world are also great listeners. Great listeners gather wisdom, insight, and discernment. They make great leaders and teachers. "Listen to advice and accept discipline [instruction], and at the end you will be counted among the wise" (Proverbs 19:20).

And maybe most importantly, teaching our children to listen to us is the beginning of teaching them to listen to God.

> *The shepherd walks right up to the gate. The gatekeeper opens the gate to him and the sheep recognize his voice. He calls his own sheep by name and leads them out. When he gets them all out, he leads them and they follow because they are familiar with his voice. They won't follow a stranger's voice but will scatter because they aren't used to the sound of it (John 10:2-5 MSG).*

Reaching Their Hearts

Maybe you are feeling like you haven't done a great job training your child to listen to you. One of my most favorite things about God is that it's never too late with Him. It's never too late to change or to do things differently with your children. It's not too late to engage the glazed-over teenager or to begin getting more than "Uh-huh" from your sons. You may have to be more strategic at this stage, consistent with your efforts and creative in your approach, but how great would it be to become the mom our kids learn to listen to?

I know you've learned a thing or two on this journey called life. Teach your kids to listen to you and pass on the wisdom.

50

Kids Need Their Mom...

To Teach Them to Not Be Easily Offended

D*on't take everything so personally. The whole world is not out to get you. Probably no one woke up this morning and said to themselves, "I'm gonna try to hurt her feelings today." Maybe your friend had a headache, or the sun was in their eyes when you thought they were smirking, or maybe they just reacted too soon. But whatever, do not be quick to take offense. And you know what? If your friend intentionally tried to offend you today, then too bad for them. We've got better things to do than be offended today. Let's forgive 'em and move on.*

No one in this family can count how many times I have given a little sermon like that. Oh, how I want my kids to get this. Do not waste your life being offended and especially when the other person meant no offense. Arrrgh. How I wish the whole world would get this!

The truth is we are all going to encounter difficult people and difficult situations, but the way we view them determines our response. Every time we embrace our "right" to be offended, even though we may actually have been mistreated, we create a division in our relationship and an opportunity for Satan to tell us lies about the situation or the person.

There are times for a righteous anger in a situation, but we have to teach our children the difference between righteous anger and harmful offense. I want my children to feel a deep anger over the atrocities of this world. I want them to feel an emotion that moves them to care more deeply and respond in maturity. I want them to know when to take up a righteous offense to defend the cause of Christ and when to lay down their offense in order to become more like Christ.

Every weekend I have the privilege of meeting women from all over the world. Several years ago, I realized that too many of the women I was meeting were living in ongoing bitterness. I understood why they felt entitled to bitterness because of divorce, health issues, or the loss of career, opportunities, friendships, and children, but at the same time, I kept asking myself, *Aren't we supposed to live differently than this?* The Bible says:

> See to it that no one falls short of the grace of God and that no bitter root grows up to cause trouble and defile many (Hebrews 12:15).

According to the Bible, bitterness is dangerous because it can take root deep inside our hearts and grow, spreading its poison into our minds and emotions before we even realize what has happened. The person who is easily offended has given their heart permission to let the root of bitterness grow. Holding on to resentments. Counting their grievances. Building grudges and bad feelings. Whenever I meet a woman who has learned to find her comfort in bitterness, I quickly pray, *Oh, Lord, keep me from such a miserable life.*

I want my children to learn to trust God when they feel offended.

I don't think the grown women I have met just recently learned how to be offended; I have a feeling they fell into a pattern early in their lives. For some reason, taking offense gave them a false sense of comfort. That's what I don't want for my children. Even at the earliest age, I don't want any of them to find a comfort in bitterness and offense.

We have a daughter in middle school. As you well know, middle-school girls are inclined toward the dramatic. Maybe one girl sat at the wrong lunch table, or another one posted a picture that left someone out. Whatever that day's new frustration, I am begging my 13-year-old daughter not to get into the game. Don't be quick to find offense. Lay down your judgment. Turn away from the gossip. Do not add flame to the fires of gossip. Be the girl who stomps it out. My daughter has to learn now what it means to overcome the temptation to be offended. I am trying to teach her:

It's okay to admit you are hurt. Let's pray about it.

Forgive the person who has offended you.

Don't keep rehashing what they did and what you should
    have done.

Be a big sister to some of the other girls. Pray for them.

Ask to be forgiven when you have been the offender.

I want my children to learn to trust God when they feel offended. He is the judge. He makes things right in His time. He reveals truth, in His way, on His terms. We need to own any part of a difficult situation that is our responsibility. Seek to restore all relationships by way of forgiveness. And then let God handle the rest. To allow ourselves to be easily offended is a self-absorbed character trait.

Our children will learn to lay down their offense or to pick it up mostly because of the way we live our lives. My dad has always given people the benefit of the doubt. Many times as a young girl, I'd try to work up an anger or offense against someone. I'd say something like, "Gosh, the clerk at that store was grumpy today. She was really short with me and almost threw my change across the counter." Ever faithful to speak from his good heart, my dad would redirect me, "Oh, Angela, you never know what that woman is dealing with. Maybe she doesn't have enough money to buy food for her family. Maybe her husband yelled at her before she left for work. Or maybe her car broke down, and she had to walk to work in the rain. I'm sure she didn't mean it toward you." Daddy had this way, still does, of dissolving the possibility of offense, turning the whole story around and making you care about the offender.

Reaching Their Hearts

May our children live free. Free from a list of offenses. Free from the chains of bitterness. Free to forgive and love and move on with their lives for the glory of God!

51

Kids Need Their Mom...

To Live as Single Moms with Amazing Lives

I lived seven years as a single mom, so it's impossible for me to write this book to moms without a special shout-out to all of you. How I wish I could give you a big hug right now. And a long vacation. A fridge full of groceries. A nicely mowed lawn. Girl, I know you are worn out. I remember my single-mom years with such fierce, still-present emotion. That was the hardest, most exhausting, and loneliest time of my life.

And yet, I want you to know, living seven years as a single mom was one of the most powerful, life-changing, make-me-a-better-person, awful things that could have ever happened.

> Where God is, you and I can still live amazing lives, full of purpose and power, for the glory of the One who has saved us!

When I became divorced, it felt like I had officially been disqualified from living. Surviving was still allowed, but living a great big life, with great big dreams? It seemed like that opportunity was gone. One day I woke up in my same pain, with my same kids, and all my same embarrassment and shame, and this question came to me: "Given these circumstances, and these wounds, and all the mess, how *now* will I live for the glory of God?" I think that question changed everything for me.

I guess I spent months asking God what He does with broken women and broken families and broken hearts. After searching the Bible, months in counseling, prayers with pastors and church elders, and long nights of holding my kids, I know the Lord came to me and very clearly told me a few things:

> I had been beautiful to Him before I was created. Nothing had changed.

> God knew before I was born that I would need a Savior. He was not surprised that I could not save my kids or myself. We needed a Savior.

> God was still on the throne, and all His promises were still good.

> God shows off His glory against the backdrop of pain.

> When broken women are redeemed and miracles happen, people look at Him and believe.

I had taken plenty of time to grieve. I had wallowed in months of insecurity and pain. When that question finally came to me, I eventually found my answer in a firm commitment to God and to my children—"I want to live an amazing life for the glory of God."

Here's what I believe. When a woman believes in God, when the Holy Spirit lives inside of her, when she has dedicated her heart and her home to follow hard after Jesus Christ, then that woman can put the full weight of her hope onto the strong promises of God. Where God is, you and I can still live amazing lives, full of purpose and power, for the glory of the One who has saved us!

I also firmly believe that God's power to save, redeem, and restore trumps all the statistics the doomsayers can throw at us. The books might say that our kids will turn out to be criminals, but where God is, I believe there is an amazing life yet to be lived! I want to encourage you to stay close to God in these years. He has all the answers you will need. He will provide strength to cover your weakness. He has been my provider, healer, confidant, and friend. Let the kids see you growing spiritually. Trust God in front of them and watch your faith give security and hope to their tender hearts.

One of the best things I did as a single mom was to keep my kids in church. I made them go to everything—Sunday morning, Wednesday night, early morning Bible study. If the youth pastor could dream it up, my kid was going to be there. Sometimes I had to hock the farm to make sure they got to every camp and retreat and mission trip, but I'd do it all over again if I had to. Church was one of the most right things happening for us in those years. Connections to godly pastors, adults, and friends became a consistent source of growth and encouragement for all of us.

With all my heart, I just want you to know that you are not alone. God has not abandoned you or your children. Give every piece of your life to Him. Dedicate your finances, the way you use your home, your private life, and especially the children to the Lord. I testify to you, and if I could type louder, I would, God is faithful! He truly does bless a life of integrity. He really does heal broken hearts. He brings prodigal children home. He breaks addictions. He changes circumstances. He gives new dreams.

Reaching Their Hearts

Oh, my sister, I am so very sorry you have to walk this path, but I don't want you to give up. More than anything, your kids need you to decide that God's promises still hold for you too. They need you to determine to abide in His presence. They deserve your intentional choice to be the very best version of mom that you can be. If for no one else but your children, will you decide to live, from this day forward, an amazing life for the glory of God?

I leave you with the passage of Scripture that gave strength to my soul and still gives me an unshakeable hope:

> *I keep asking that the God of our Lord Jesus Christ, the glorious Father, may give you the Spirit of wisdom and revelation, so that you may know him better. I pray that the eyes of your heart may be enlightened in order that you may know the hope to which he has called you, the riches of his glorious inheritance in his holy people, and his incomparably great power for us who believe (Ephesians 1:17-19).*

All God's promises for you still hold. Build your life on His faithfulness, and go live an amazing life for His glory!

52

Kids Need Their Mom...

To Teach Them a Gracious and Generous Hospitality

My grandmother's voice rings in my head—

> *Angela, run get the neighbor a glass of tea. It's hot enough to faint.*
>
> *Children, come up here on the porch and rest for a minute.*
>
> *Bring your family for dinner and stay as long as you can.*
>
> *We're having such a good time, why don't you just spend the night?*
>
> *I'll add another potato to the soup. We'll have plenty.*
>
> *It's better to have a little together than a lot alone.*

Little did I know that she was handing down beautiful words of hospitality that would be written across my heart for a lifetime. Someone has said that hospitality is the process of receiving outsiders and changing them from strangers to guests. I love that. The Bible speaks often about the practice of hospitality. Not only is hospitality an expression of Christian faith, it is also an outworking of love. To serve with a gracious and generous hospitality is to let the love of Christ flow out of us onto our families, friends, and those strangers who will become guests.

Company's coming! I loved those words as a little girl, and I still love them today. I am truly the happiest when every bed is full and I'm stepping over people in the morning. I love the energy, the laughter, and the undeniable warmth that fills our home. People love being loved on, and boy, do I enjoy doing that.

My 17-year-old called last Saturday afternoon and said, "Can I have some people come over tonight?"

"Sure, honey, just let us know when you're coming and about how many," we said.

"Oh, I think we have about 12 people, and we'll be there for dinner."

I know it sounds crazy, but we loved having 12 teenagers for dinner at the last minute. I yelled, "Company's coming!" and we all jumped into fun gear. We were off to the store for some food and snacks. We lit the candles and built a fire. Turned on all the lights. Found just the right cool, teenage, boy music. Put out the plates and napkins and readied ourselves for laughter and fun. Half of them went home later and half of them spent the night. Woohoo! Pancakes were flying for breakfast the next morning.

Kids know when you enjoy having them around. Actually, most people can tell if they are welcome, but I think hospitality goes one step past welcoming. With hospitality there is a come-as-you-are acceptance accompanied by a gracious generosity. It's really hard to be hospitable when you are judgmental and stingy.

One of the sweetest things we can do is to save our best stuff for sharing. Who in the world wants to eat an expensive box of chocolates all alone? That makes absolutely no sense to me. Wonderful chocolate is for sharing! Hospitality means unclenching your hands and generously bestowing the gifts of your time, your talents, and your affection. Years ago a family invited us for dinner. The mom prepared each plate, and the kids turned to me holding a plate with their tiny portion of chicken, part of a potato, and a spoonful of beans. Now I completely understand that there are times when you have only a little to share, but honestly, I was there and that was not the case in this home. They had plenty but gave rations for dinner. Needless to say, we had to stop and feed the boys on the way home. I think that if you'd rather be stingy, it's okay not to have people over. Hospitality is warm and generous and filling.

I like for our guests to sleep on the best sheets and use the good towels and unwrap the little soaps for their bath. We have a guest room, and I pray in there all the time. I pray for the last person who slept there and for the yet unknown guest who will arrive. I ask that our home would be a place of rest and comfort. When I was finally able to buy a bed to use for guests, my friend lay down on it and said, "This bed is too comfortable. After people sleep on this, they are going to want to stay longer." Honestly, I kind of thought that was the point. I want their bed to be comfy and the bathrobes hanging in their room to be snuggly. I truly believe we are supposed to bless people with our homes, our food, and the sharing of our things.

This year I heard the story of a family who at Thanksgiving realized they had enough food to feed six more people. So they posted a notice on a website saying they had room at their table for six more if anyone needed a place to go. They had to take down the posting after 36 people responded they had no where to go and no money to buy a meal. This gracious family, so moved by the responders, invited all 36 to lunch. I was moved to tears and moved to imitate them. I bet we could have fed 20 more with our leftovers last year.

> Sweet hospitality is little bit addictive. Your family will begin to love the way it makes them feel to bless others with kindness and sharing.

It's the best mom gift to watch my children practice hospitality with their friends. Anna-Grace will lay out a bath towel for her friends or put out an assortment of snacks in the kitchen. The boys even get in on all the action, and one will sweep the porch while the other lights all the lanterns. Sweet hospitality is little bit addictive. Your family will begin to love the way it makes them feel to bless others with kindness and sharing.

Reaching Their Hearts

Hospitality is not some kind of specialized spiritual gift that only a few people possess. The Bible says we are supposed to "offer hospitality to one another without grumbling" (1 Peter 4:9). I think that passage is for all believers. So what do you say? Let's open our hearts and teach our children to receive others into our lives with a hospitable spirit that is generous and good. And above all this, let us imitate the love of Christ and His hospitality to all we meet.

More Great Harvest House Books
by Angela Thomas

Prayers for My Baby Boy
Text by Angela Thomas
Photography by Julie Johnson

Awesome. Breathtaking. Stunning. Surely, he is the most amazing gift I have ever known. Now there is a new life in our home. Thank You, God, for answering our prayers. I can look into the eyes of our gift and see his daddy's reflection. I am so humbled. I never could have dreamed what this day would be like. I am a mother, he is my child, and we are home. Amen.

Beautiful prayers and wonderful photographs make this hardcover, four-color book a joy to read, look at, and give as gifts. Each prayer, presented as a letter to God, celebrates a mom's delight in everyday moments with a newborn boy. Each expression of hope, gratitude, and purpose is beautifully bundled with Julie Johnson's heartwarming photos of sweet babies that are sure to spark smiles. From the very first page, you'll be reminded of the many joys and privileges of raising a child and be led to times of prayer and thanksgiving. This tender tribute to the wonders of new life and the divine gift of motherhood also makes a perfect keepsake for moms, grandmas, aunts, and anyone who treasures little ones.

Prayers for My Baby Girl

Text by Angela Thomas

Photography by Julie Johnson

I feel keenly aware that my life will never be the same. Yet I wouldn't go back for all the treasure in the world. How did I ever live without her? Thank You, sweet Lord, for the immeasurable gift of our baby. "Your works are wonderful, I know that full well." Hallelujah. Amen.

With heartfelt prayers written as letters to God and winsome photos of babies, *Prayers for My Baby Girl* will touch your heart and help you praise God for the wonders of motherhood. The beautiful thoughts of joy and hope are accompanied by the full-color photographs of sweet and cute babies. This hardcover book makes a perfect gift for moms, grandmas, aunts, and anyone who delights in babies.

The Story of Your Life
Matthew West and Angela Thomas

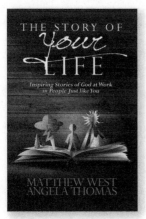

When Grammy-nominated recording artist Matthew West invited people to share their stories, he received nearly 10,000 responses. As he read every one, entering into other people's joy, pain, and hope in God, his heart was transformed. Eleven of the accounts inspired the songs on his bestselling *The Story of Your Life* album.

Now Matthew and his friend and fellow author Angela Thomas respond to 52 of those stories. Each brief reading includes a story, Scripture passages, and Matthew or Angela's compassionate and insightful response, revealing how God is at work in each situation. You'll read about...

- Wendy, the unmarried woman who gave birth to her daughter while in jail, and how God turned her life around.

- Kristen, the foster girl who is about to turn 18 and has nowhere to go, and how she discovered that God is her true Father.

- Greg, the pastor whose congregation lined the streets with banners and cheers as he and his wife brought home Lily, the little girl they adopted from Guatemala.

In these inspiring glimpses into people's lives, you'll see how God is at work in everyone's story—including yours.